Produce Wagon

Ted Kooser Contemporary Poetry   EDITOR: Ted Kooser

Produce Wagon

New and Selected Poems

ROY SCHEELE

Introduction by Ted Kooser

University of Nebraska Press · Lincoln

Acknowledgments for the use of copyrighted
material appear on pages xiii–xv, which constitute
an extension of the copyright page.

The University of Nebraska Press is part of a land-
grant institution with campuses and programs on the
past, present, and future homelands of the Pawnee,
Ponca, Otoe-Missouria, Omaha, Dakota, Lakota, Kaw,
Cheyenne, and Arapaho Peoples, as well as those of the
relocated Ho-Chunk, Sac and Fox, and Iowa Peoples.

Library of Congress Control Number: 2021048481

Designed and set in Garamond Premier Pro by L. Auten.

For Francy,
as always

A promise depends on what occurs.
But the first star I see tonight is yours.

What would the world be, once bereft
Of wet and of wildness? Let them be left,
O let them be left, wildness and wet;
Long live the weeds and the wilderness yet.

—Gerard Manley Hopkins, "Inversnaid"

CONTENTS

New Poems

ACKNOWLEDGMENTS

The dedicatory couplet to my wife, Francy, entitled "If It Clears," originally appeared in *Grams and Epigrams*, a Triptych Broadside, © 1973 by Roy Scheele.

A word of explanation regarding "Keeping the Horses," which first appeared in *The Sea-Ocean*, my third collection, in 1981. The poem was also published in *Pointing Out the Sky*, the following collection (1985), and later as a chapbook from Windflower Press in 1998, as well as in several anthologies in the interval. In the mid-1980s I wrote a pendant poem, "The Lookout," which appeared in *Prairie Schooner* in 1990. I printed the two poems together as "The Carny Circuit" in *A Far Allegiance* in 2010 and do so again here in order to avoid confusion for a reader who may have read "Keeping the Horses" in one of its earlier appearances.

Previous Publication Credits

"Remembrances," "The Welcome Mat," "Flowering Crab," "At Brim on the Little Blue," "Rock Openings," "A Metaphor for the Evening Star," and "The Gap in the Cedar" from *Accompanied* (Crete NE: Best Cellar Press). © 1974 by Roy Scheele.

"Noticing," "A Kitchen Memory," "Fishing Blue Creek," "Poppies," "August," "Missing You," "What Swept by on a Winter Morning," and "How the Fox Got Away" from *Noticing* (Lincoln NE: Three Sheets Press). © 1979 by Roy Scheele.

"The Sea-Ocean," "Spring Greens," "Nebraska U.S. 20," "The Falls," "Focal Point," "A Turn in the Weather," "Winter Onions," "Remembering Anna," and "Grandpa Mac" from *The Sea-Ocean*, in *Close to Home: Poems*, ed. Fredrick Zydek, The Annex 21: American Poetry series, no. 3 (Omaha NE: University of Nebraska at Omaha). *The Sea-Ocean* © 1981 by Roy Scheele.

"Watching You Open Your New, Many-Hued Umbrella" from *The Sledders: Thirty Sonnets* (Lincoln NE: Three Sheets Press). © 2016 by Roy Scheele.

Some of the new poems and uncollected poems have been previously printed in the following journals/anthologies: *Arts & Letters, Commonweal, Forty Nebraska Poets* (Crete NE: Best Cellar Press, 1981), *Going Over to Your Place* (New York: Bradbury Press, 1987), *The Lyric, Measure: A Review of Formal Poetry, Nebraska Poetry: A Sesquicentennial Anthology 1867–2017* (Nacogdoches TX: Stephen F. Austin State University Press, 2017), *The New Formalist, Northeast, The Rockford Review,* and *Watching the Perseids: The Backwaters Press Twentieth Anniversary Anthology* (Omaha NE: Backwaters Press, 2017).

The following poems first appeared in *Prairie Schooner*: "Dakota Burial," *Prairie Schooner* 53, no. 3 (Fall 1979); "Househunting," *Prairie Schooner* 58, no. 2 (Summer 1984); "The Hadderways," *Prairie Schooner* 84, no. 2 (Summer 2010); "Cover of Darkness," *Prairie Schooner* 79, no. 4 (Winter 2005). © University of Nebraska Press.

Other credits include *Alicorn, The American Scholar, Black Willow Poetry, The Bloomsbury Review, The Blue Hotel, Cedar Rock, The Decade Dance* (Sandhills Press), *English Journal, Hurakan: A Journal of Contemporary Literature, Leaves of Grass, Lucid Rhythms, Nebraska English and Language Arts Journal, The New Salt Creek Reader, Pebble, Pivot, Plainsong, Plainsongs, Poetry, Public Herald, The Road Not Taken, The Sandhills & Other Geographies, The Sewanee Review, The Small Farm, Southern Humanities Review, The Southern Review, Tennessee Poetry Journal, Texas Poetry Journal, Whole Notes,* and *Wind.*

Thanks to all of these publications for permission to reprint the poems included here, and particularly to those editors who published my chapbooks and full-length books or opened the pages of their magazines to me: Greg Kuzma, the late Fred Zydek, Mark Sanders, the late John Judson, Nancy Peters Hastings, Greg Kosmicki, Frank Steele, Jeff Daniel Marion, the late John Fandel, Rob Griffith, Paul Bone, and Hilda Raz. Most of all, my gratitude to Ted Kooser for his unfailing support over the years.

The University of Nebraska Press has been very generous to me by permitting me to bring before readers the life work of American poets whom I greatly admire, and, in this instance, have admired for more than fifty years—admired, delighted in, respected, and been deeply moved by. This collection of new and selected poems by Roy Scheele is the seventh book in my series.

To say that Scheele is a poet's poet might suggest that his writing is by intent directed toward that one small and exclusive audience and not for a more general reader, but that's not at all what I mean. If we look at the poems of, say, Robert Frost or Elizabeth Bishop or Richard Wilbur—and I'm confident Roy Scheele belongs in their company—we might say of them, too, that they are poet's poets, but that's only to state that poets can learn from reading them. To show how poems can and may be written is one small helpful service for a poet to offer, but we all know that it's the great beauty and deep humanity of Bishop and Frost and Wilbur that keep everyday readers returning to them.

The book you're holding offers all those qualities, beauty and humanity and exemplary writing.

And music, too, or "having an ear," a quality increasingly rare in contemporary poetry.

People who were taught in school to read words as representations of thoughts find it difficult to hear the sounds of words, and I feel sorry for them. I feel even sorrier for them when they try to write poems, because their words seem unaware of the sound they're making, so that their poems are flat constructions of thoughts, missing perhaps as much as a third of their potential effect.

In the late Clive James's final book, *The Fire of Joy*, he says this of poetry: "Noise, I believe, is the first and last thing poetry is. . . . With a poem the most important thing is the way it sounds when you say it. At that rate even the most elementary nursery rhyme has it all over the kind of overstuffed epic that needs 10 pages of notes for every page of text, and reduces all who read it to paralyzed slumber—or even worse, to a bogus admiration."

Here follows an example of what James is talking about in regard to sound, and which I find everywhere among the poems of Roy Scheele. Poems with music, poems made of music, show up very early in Scheele's work and are with us all the way through his career as a writer. This poem, for example, comes quite early in *Produce Wagon* and foretells the music to be a part of Scheele's many years of fine writing:

Flowering Crab
The blossoms are gone, down to the last one,
and now the tree stands clear in russet leaves
as if to make articulate on high
the rush of things beyond them. How shyly
the leaves brush up against the blue, with each
delicate adjustment of a leaf
stemming from the same tree source, a wholeness,
as a long look will pass from face to face
and a touch lean out for the lines of a cheek.
Here is the tree's unhurried color, here
its true identity, and all the rest
persiflage, camouflage, bunting, the blur
of the oriole in the upper branches.
Lightly the tree adjusts to a sense of its loss.

How many words in "Flowering Crab" make the sound of a tree, its leaves rustling? Look at the deft use of all of those *s* sounds. Here we have a poem about a tree that actually sounds like a tree! As I write this, a flowering crab that's about fifty feet from me is making those same sounds. That's what Clive James is looking for and what you'll find throughout this book. And in few other books of poetry being published today.

When asked what kind of poet she thought herself to be, Elizabeth Bishop said she was "a descriptive poet." "Flowering Crab" deftly and evocatively shows us a tree. A poem of description is a gift, and the more true and evocative the description the more significant gift it is. For one of us to go somewhere and come back to tell the rest of us what he or she saw out there in the world is an ancient activity, something our remotest ancestors were doing gathered by fires at the mouths of caves. We see a group like those ancestors in Scheele's poem "Salon Noir, Niaux." What we now call literature descends from those long-ago storytelling moments.

You're holding a book of many poems of description, but also of narratives in Scheele's voice, and in imagined voices. There are poems of single, fleeting moments rendered beautifully in lyric forms, sonnets, free verse, blank verse, with mastery in all of these. I'll close with just one of the many poems I rank with the best of those of our distinguished forebears, Housman, Hardy, Bishop, and others, a poem with not one extra part, not one word that doesn't contribute to its effect, and all of it delivered gracefully:

Changing the Flowers
In the newer cemetery, south of town,
the markers barely show above the ground—
the marble bolsters of eternal sleep.
Only the plastic flowers in their urns
keep up the memory across the years
of daisies in a glass beside the bed,
and someone lifted from the pillows there
with someone else's hand beneath his head.

Produce Wagon

From *Accompanied*, 1974

Remembrances

The cardinal in her nest in the bare forsythia
is for your mother, by which to remember
that lucid evening she pointed it out to me
from where she stood at the window.

For myself I choose the hawk and that winter
day I turned from reading the face of the stream
and was gathered up in its eyes.

And for you, the little bat we rumpled with our
breathing as we crowded round its sleep
on the side of the oak tree the evening we moved in
here: not a bird, but a mammal
whose sight is its flight, on wings
no wider than the spread of my hand.

The Welcome Mat

Having spun a web out of herself,
an exacting string,
the spider waits to see if the moonlight
can cross to her safe on that footing.

Flowering Crab

The blossoms are gone, down to the last one,
and now the tree stands clear in russet leaves
as if to make articulate on high
the rush of things beyond them. How shyly
the leaves brush up against the blue, with each
delicate adjustment of a leaf
stemming from the same tree source, a wholeness,
as a long look will pass from face to face
and a touch lean out for the lines of a cheek.
Here is the tree's unhurried color, here
its true identity, and all the rest
persiflage, camouflage, bunting, the blur
of the oriole in the upper branches.
Lightly the tree adjusts to a sense of its loss.

At Brim on the Little Blue

You would remember this: one summer evening
in the cabin clearing high above where the river
stole away in timber and clay at our feet.
The water working its shoulders, all silt, down under
the silk of the flow, a calm, rambling sheen. And the sunset:
it lay on the water just at the bend where the river
crooked an elbow and was gone, gone with it too
the gesture you said it completed downstream, a swirl
on the silence, fingers stretched out for the last
reaches of light. The silence went so deep in us then,
and the light, only the right word could have forded them.
We stood a long time like that, our gaze flung wide
for that listening, till darkness came over the river,
then threw the one last look over our shoulders
coming back. Still deep: our hands touched, we trembled.

Rock Openings

1 Geode with Grape Cluster Surface

One agate, cloven, opens on a cave
of crystals brimming like a bunch of grapes
fanned out against the ceiling's smoky reach,
the bottom of the cluster blurred with frost,
and in its fastnesses, not wholly formed,
grape embryos likely to come out breach
move counterclockwise in a show of heads
bowed neatly from the nape, a pin of light
set in the skull like the vestigial
eyespot, the pulse of the pineal gland,
drawing a thin second skin over the dull ripening.

2 Slabbed Blue Agate

These, struck apart and held against the sky
so that a summer cloud shows through between,
might easily be taken for the lobes
of the lungs, or maybe the fossil wings
of some longlost, exotic butterfly.
On the lobe or wing on the left's an eye,
a blue as placid as a mountain lake,
a thing seen to advantage from on high,
while on the right a slightly smaller lobe
varies the markings from the other side,
a deep meandering of darks and lights
where one by one valley, peak, and basin
grind crystal after crystal into place.
And yet the hands that heave them into view,
one would suppose, know something after all:
they have them lightly by the fingertips,
as if they lifted two unwrinkling wings.

3 Dendritic (Moss) Opal

And this one's like an acorn cracked in two,
rot at it from its lying on the ground,
excepting that the thing has petrified
and bears a dark potential knot of leaves,
close underfoot, down to the end of time.
Make every bit as much of little here
as you may like, it seems no more a tree
than does the pit you pluck and toss away
out of the peach's sweet and grasping reach. Oh,
nothing on God's green earth ever wants to let go!
But since the name implants a metaphor,
this tree that sprang, ages ago, in stone,
bids us come closer for a second look.
And look! It is a tree that's been cut down,
with all that milling darkness centered on
the effort to come out into its own:
now you can tell it is a ring of ants
sacking a city of larvae and grubs,
their bodies led by hunger in a dance—
the surface of the stump just crawls with them.

A Metaphor for the Evening Star

You rise up in a gap of sky between
two mountains, looking every inch a pearl—
as if the sky had spun itself for days
around a grain that gathered in its side.

The Gap in the Cedar

in memory of my father

I saw this much from the window:
the branch spring lightened into place
with a lithe shudder of snow.

Whatever bird had been there,
chickadee or sparrow,
had so vanished into air,

resilient, beyond recall,
it had to be taken on faith
to be taken at all.

In the moment it took the tree
to recover that trembling
something went wide in me—

there was a rush of wings,
the air beaten dim with snow,
and then I saw through the swirling.

From *Noticing*, 1979

Noticing

I've been wanting all day
to show you this: how much
the fallen tulip petals
resemble scorpion tails,
the stamens bent back
and pinched in a half inch
below the tip.

        There's a small
black tulip, the shadow
of one, its shape, draped
over the inner edge
of each petal. See?
It's like the long stain
of the sun on a dial.

Look with me for a while.

A Kitchen Memory

My mother is paring an apple over the sink,
her two deft hands effortless and intent.
The skin comes away in the shape of a corkscrew,
red and white by turns, with a shimmer of rose
where the blade in its turn cuts close: a blush,
called out of hiding like a second skin.
Now the apple fattens in her hand;
the last scrap of parings falls away;
and she halves and sections the white grainy meat,
picks up another apple, brushes back
the dark hair at her temple with the knife hand.
The only sound is the fan stirring the heat.

Fishing Blue Creek

(in Tennessee, with my brother Tom, 1968)

That pair of great blue herons,
as shy as two low touching clouds
where the bend gave out in glitter,
was gone almost before we knew it,
wheeling and banking above the trees
and heading downstream against the sun.
The minnows skittered in the shallows
for a long time afterwards.
The light went wading on its own.

Poppies

The light in them stands as clear as water
drawn from a well.
When the breeze moves across them they totter.
You half expect them to spill.

August

In waves of heat
        beside the road
                the field is all

striation,
        a wet shimmer
                drawn on the air—

nothing but grass,
        and the goldenrod
                going to waste

with abandon,
        a paste of yellows,
                wading uphill.

Missing You

Your voice tonight came in across the miles
of looping wire as clear and sure (though far)
as the small dipping gleam above the car
when daylight swings between the startled poles.

What Swept by on a Winter Morning

A paper bag
came bounding down the street
toward us as we drove,
caught up on the wind
by its open end,
a tumbleweed motion
that flattened and filled again.

Just by watching
I knew the sound of it,
even with windows
shut tight on the cold:
that flap, lifted up,
bellied out on the wind,
slapping the air as it dove.

How the Fox Got Away

That evening it was so still
you could hear a shadow.
That's how I came to see her
when she slipped out from the tree,
stumbling a little, hauling
at the deep veins of her kill.
I felt the light between us
lean down across the pasture
for her ear, combing sound
out of a strand of fur. She turned
then, and for a moment
drew off my breath in her gaze.
Then she was gone.

Leaving behind her meal. At the foot
of the hill I found it—a young
possum, its throat let out in a wide
scarf of blood—and the path
she turned in on through the rye. A yard
back from the fence it veered away
toward the swamp, lost there
in the dazzle of new grain,
mist rising from the field now
and out of the mist, the moon.

From *The Sea-Ocean*, 1981

The Sea-Ocean

My son's name for it, that strand across which
everyone lives in a far-off land. We will go
there one day and see it, I tell him,
proud and offhand.

The sea. Here in Nebraska thousands of years ago
one dove down forever beneath our feet,
so that now we walk on the water's deep shoulders
when we walk down the street. The Platte
walks down the Missouri into the Mississippi and
steps off into the sea, as you and I
might walk into a store. And the ocean
is where seas meet.

It is raining as I tell this over your sleep
that puts out on the waves of the thunder,
lashed to the breaking deck of what we are—
mere flesh and bone the water
will try to pull under. We were sailors
from the womb, and have come far:
each day we live is over another deep.

Spring Greens

for Steve and Dana Gehring

1 Chive

It has wintered well.
There where the grass meets the garden,
the black of the fresh-turned soil,
its rounded, gray-green stems
splay like a fountain—
labor, and rest from labor,
caught in an equipoise.

2 Parsley

There's nothing left,
so we start from seed:
each is brown, and hard
as a lacquered bead.

A handful soaked
in an old shot glass
(turned, overnight,
to a cloudy brass)

now lies in the earth
in a dark reversion,
putting down roots.
Their own dispersion

turned for the Jews
to memories kept,
and the crinkly green,
salt-water-dipped,

serves to remind
at the *seder* meal
how the tears that blind
may also heal.

3 Dill

Two delicate blades,
and then two more, until the border
is thick with them as a bank of oars
bent slightly by the water round a ship.
Such a faint shimmering! barely green
from a few feet off, more like a mist
cleared from the sides by the morning sun.

Thriving on neglect,
the dill has seeded itself and raised
this haven from the winter storms.

The seedlings crowd like sailors up on deck.

Nebraska U.S. 20

We've been driving all day toward heat waves
that turn into oases of the dead,
small bodies darkening the road ahead,
feathers and clots of fur against the glare—
what the Highway Department calls "nocturnals."

This morning, near Crookston, I braked and slowed
for a weasel shambling across the road,
his short front legs stooping him over,
his long back fur on end as if a wave
were breaking there, pitching him clear of the car.

The Falls

After the walk down to the river,
the ride across on a cable car
worked by a hand winch on either shore
(or the one inside you operate
yourself, cranking along the wire),
taking the path through the meadow
with its one fly-pestered friendly horse,
the house up there behind a screen of trees,
the sideyard littered with old cars
and the stacked and shiny bales of straw
where a speckled rooster struts and cries,
cocking the head his echo magnifies;
after you've ducked through a round wire fence
and left your prints where you leaped the creek,
crossing to climb on the other side,
beyond the campers' blue nylon tents
pegged out like patches of fallen sky
and the lesser falls like a spillway
out from under a bridge of ties,
the climb becoming much steeper now,
ringed in by trees, the way worn out
of the chalky, porous soil, the bark
of a birch branch lying in tatters
below a pool, light reaching down
through leaves to sway above the gravel,
brightening and fading like a glancing trout,
the sound of the falls now standing out
above the stream, the breeze-cascading leaves,
till the path, suddenly deflecting
hard to the left, brings on a clearing,
and you come to what you've come to see:
the current riding in a shattered veil
over the rock face, the rim a crown

of trees, the rippled white of birches,
the water-darkened wall dim as a hearth.
On the face of it the stone is scored,
or hollowed into brimming basins;
the moss lets down a curtain of beads.
Up close, you can even feel the mist.
Taking each other's picture, you stand back,
wanting that dazzle focused and drawn tight
by a dear face, in a familiar light.

Focal Point

And this one you took, lopping off
the top half of my head. I loom,
like the stem of a mushroom,
and smile for all that is left between us,
for better or worse, unsaid.

See, I'm holding the baby, but it's more
a likeness of you: out of these years
of marriage, yet one more proof
how love goes with us here,
with you still on the shy side
of the camera, letting the light leak through.

Some evening, over coffee,
we'll get out the album and bare
this moment to someone's eyes—
and someone, astonished at hearing
us have such fun at mechanics' expense,
is sure to say, "It's good of the baby,"
and sip and look away.

A Turn in the Weather

(Calder's mobile *Roxbury Flurry*)

oh
the slow
downsifting
eddying fall
of snow!

the flakes
wet white
but light
as air
uplifted now

barely astir
against
the wall
circling in
shadow

a swirl
of light
moving in place
while falling still
somehow

Winter Onions

They hang from a rafter
in the basement
like bells on a string,

crackly as parchment,
about the size
of tulip bulbs at planting.

The skins are a pale bronze
whose ringing awaits
the paring knife,

the tears at the core of things,
a swirl of green and white
where the clapper swings.

Tethered to darkness
under the joists,
they gather down the dust

as in a loft;
the skins break and flake off,
imitating peals.

Remembering Anna

Her hands in the dough,
she would fold and slap it
like a baby's rump,
then roll it out
into bread and kolaches.

Thanksgiving with her
was duck and goose
and giblet gravy,
dumplings and yams
and the sweet Czech sauerkraut.

Married at just fifteen,
she gave it everything—
the kids, the deepening years,
and then the end—
the cinch of the wedding ring.

Grandpa Mac

That strip of cornhusk
blown up from the field,
grappling with light
on the barbed wire,

stood in my mind
for his duress,
the final illness
dreaming him back

across the years
to the Kansas farm.
When we drove back,
it was gone.

From *Pointing Out the Sky*, 1985

Making Change

How old was I then, about five?
I'm standing in Miller & Paine,
the gleaming department store
at the very center of town,
wearing a sailor suit
and clutching my mother's hand.
Something that brought us here—
some long-forgotten errand,
a pair of gloves or a scarf—
has glued my eyes to the glass
of an immaculate case,
beyond which rises a tall
cream-pale plaster column
with Corinthian capital.
The skin of one sweaty leg
is chafing against the starch,
the pressed white hem, of my shorts.
Now Mother has made her purchase
and hands over a crispy ten;
the saleslady (no "persons" then)
takes it and folds it in half,
snaps open a cylinder
of sullen brass, with a trapdoor,
and bumpers at either end,
and tucks it in; turns with it then
and shoves it into a chute, like loading
a shell in a howitzer,
and sends it off with a *whoosh*.
She and Mother small-talk;
I stand there stricken dumb.
After a minute or two
there's a clatter and tumbling sound
and the chute has sucked it in;

it scuttles back down the pipe
and lands with a thump in a bin.
The lady opens the trapdoor;
out come the dollars and change.
"How would you like a soda?"
my mother says, and we walk
across the street to Walgreens
for two chill-sided glasses,
foam towering over their rims.

Saturday Mornings in the Radio Years

1 Tiger Salamander

Behind the water plant
there was a concrete shaft
dim as a shallow well,
with a wooden cover
like a barrel. You climbed
down an iron ladder;
the rungs rang out below,
grown colder in your grip
the further down you'd go.
Above your head the sky
had never looked so blue,
so much like water.

The last one down was first
to spot the salamander.
He held it by the tail
on the flat of his hand,
wriggling from side to side,
the cold skin sagging in
just behind its shoulders.
We climbed back up with it,
into a world so bright
its yellow markings splashed
through wave on wave of light.
I shivered touching it.

2 Substituting

I got up in the dark;
outside it was lighter.

Walking the route that morning,
the big out-of-town papers

digging into my thighs,
I cut across a lawn
and brushed against a spruce.
A mourning dove flew out
without a cry or sound
but the creak of its wings.

When I got home the dark
had welled up into blue
and thinned out overhead
like clearing water. Two
doves were calling, calling,
as I crawled back into bed;

I could hardly hear them
for the wings in my head.

3 Things as They Come

It seemed as if something
ought to be happening
in the clear morning air:
I dressed and went outside.
The dew was lying still
on the catalpa pods
I'd not yet used for swords,
on the crossed blades of grass.
My footprints left a streak,
like a slug's, where I passed.

Across the street, the sun
stood in the high windows
of the school, glinting down
onto the wet gravel
of the playground. I made
my first-light trek across
that desert stretch of sand.

Swaying in the stirrups
of bent wire mesh
on the alley fence,
I swung to the saddle
of my Arabian,
the top strand for a seat,
then, bracing on a post,
got up on the lean-to
attached to a garage.

Below me, in the pond's
dark, scum-clouded water,
a large pale-bellied goldfish
would scull and disappear
underneath the algae,
swimming around the rim
only to reappear
in a ripple of scales—
as good as a mirage.

4 Chores

My father never had
to call me more than once:
twice was unheard of.
So, on that autumn day
when I stood raking leaves
into a restive pile,
scarlet and gold and all,
and heard his voice come up
the basement passageway,
shaping my syllable,
I let the light rake fall
and started down the stairs.

He asked me if I'd seen
his level anywhere

(he had just planed a board
that could not fail to hold
the bubble steady there).
Well, no, I hadn't, but . . .
couldn't I help him look?
We hunted through the scrolls
of sweet-scented shavings
among his other tools—
and found it on its hook.
He cleared his throat, then laughed.

The Catch

(West Battle Lake, Minnesota)

Below our cabin a sandy road
that led to the general store,
the boat dock, and the other cabins
of the small, tree-set resort
dipped down into a hollow
where it crossed, ten yards from shore,
a creek whose clear, sweet water
spilled into the lake. It was here,
the day we arrived, that I knelt
and dipped my hand, and felt the pull
of the water's glide and, rising, saw,
in a pool where the creek swung round,
a drifting school of bluegills,
impossibly large and fat ones
the size of a grown man's hand.
Though a white wooden sign
forbade it (SPAWNING
BEDS/NO FISHING MAY THROUGH JUNE),
I hurried up to the cabin,
fishing my rod from the pile
of things that I'd helped to carry
in from the car (for Mother
to sort out and stow away
later that afternoon), and ran
back down to the bridge, secreting
the pole and open-face reel
beneath it, then on down the road,
through spurting sand, to the store,
where I bought a carton of mealworms
and walked back winded with them
to my cache, my furtive purpose.

I was ten years old, I knew
the difference between right and wrong,
knew from the sign that this was wrong,
yet felt a tug like the current's,
undeniably strong, and knew
(had known from the beginning)
I would bait up the wriggling hook
and let the light, shot-weighted line
drift in among them.

                It was pure Eden,
that hour of fishing! At the end of it
my rope stringer sagged with fish.
I tied it to a plank-end on the bridge,
drawing it through the loop at the other end,
so that it made a kind of wreath
of fins and tails and gills that swayed like coral,
and I went up to lunch.
Afterwards I helped with the dishes
and then, my plans gone glimmering,
was made to take a nap
in the cool back bedroom, the light
off the lake trembling on the ceiling,
translating the slap of water
in the reeds outside . . . When I awoke
it was midafternoon. I ran
to the bridge. The stringer was taut,
and looking down through the water
I saw a turtle ripping the tail
off one of the bluegills. I hauled
at the line, feeling it suddenly
give way, and up through the sun-drenched water
I drew my string of fish: half of them
only half there, ribbons of flesh
and torn pink guts come drifting up with them,

caught up like banners in the current,
and on the bridge I took them off
one by one, heads and whole fish,
and dropped them into the water.

The Farm in Arkansas

The pump on its concrete slab,
with its arm of flashing water,
so cold it burned clear through me;
the grape arbor on the south;
in the fenced-in lot by the barn
where Josey the mule hung out
up to his knees in weeds,
a harrow so long unused
its teeth were sunk deep in rust;
and the barn dark chinked with light,
the dropping-spattered floor,
hay sifting its way down through the loft
with the twitter of swallow and sparrow,
and the leather smell of the harness,
a whiff of dry sweat and urine;
walking Grandpa back from his chores
and milling around outside,
grasshoppers crackling and whirring
in the tall grass back of the house;
watching a butterfly, all white,
shoulder the sun on its wings
and stagger away in flight;
then in through the screen porch door,
the slapping back of the spring,
the radio on inside,
and there at the sink stood Grandma
up to her wrists in grapes
picked while my back was turned,
rinsing them off at the tap,
the fruit heavy and jouncing
on the bubble-juggling stems,

the big blue speckled pot
set on the front of the stove,
ready to make the jelly
she somehow knew I craved.

Uncle Lou

I remember he kept, when I was young,
a little flock of pigeons in a shed.
I would hear them chortling behind the door
as he fumbled with the latch. We'd enter
a dimness full of the richest smells—
mash and droppings, feathers and sidling dust—
the doorway lying tipped across the floor
in a light in which we stood exalted.

Once he caught one and, while cupping its wings
in his hands, let it peck at the corn
and millet that I held out to it. And that
was like him—to make you a part of things.
Today the flat of my outstretched empty hand
tingled when I heard that he was gone.

Sandhill Cranes

Why did I feel like weeping
on seeing the cranes go by?

O snowy bodies and dark-tipped wings
scudding cloudlike across the sky

(over the mud-shouldered road straggling
north as the crow flies),

you filled me with such deep longing
under your hurtling cries!

Crossing the Field

The grass starts
at my footstep
as the grasshoppers
all take wing. They

kick away
in all directions,
like a chaff
in a whirlwind

or a fire
of crackling twigs,
touching so lightly
the only sign

that they've flown
is a twitching
that keeps to the grass.
They wait en masse:

my least move
will scatter the lot
every which way
all over again,

till the field
is told over
in flower and legume
a thousand times

and they come—
just when it seems
they've run out of room—
to the end of their run.

At the Drought's Height

All night over a field
at the edge of town,
over the roof of a shed,
the Dipper that's hung
on the nail of the polestar
turns till it's upright,
the drops at its lip
dusty but gleaming,
wetting the sky with its light.

Cisterns

"Once down there," he said,
"you can hardly believe how cool they are,
even in summer. In the old days

they used them to keep ice in
for the threshing bees, big oblong blocks
the size of a hearthstone,

cutting them out on the river
in the dead of winter, chiseling and sawing
like men who quarried marble slabs.

They would snag one in a hitch of ropes,
and the horses would haul it up
the bankside with muscles straining

and their breathing like steam
in the icy air, tossing their heads
like funeral horses under a snow of plumes,

and when they had a sledful
they'd head back across the fields,
the traces and harness taut with it,

the row of cows at the fence
turning their heads as one
as the load entered the farmyard.

Then the men took up the strain,
shoving the blocks over the cistern rim
and down into the dark.

One hot July afternoon
when the wheat was in
they'd haul up a few on ropes,

the drops slicking the wagonbed,
and pulling up beside the horsetank
they'd catch a block with baling hooks

and pitch it in, and each time
the kids that stood around would shriek
and jump back from the slosh.

Then the farmers would throw in jugs of wine
and bottled beer and whisky, all that glass
and crockery bobbing around

and clinking against the ice and metal sides
like round after round of toasts.
And the drinking would go on

until nothing was left,
the women bringing coffee and sandwiches
every few hours through the night.

Always, thinking of cisterns I recall
those parties, and the joy of harvest,
and the great dark vaulting roof

and echoing sides of the one on our place,
my brother and I sent down to clean it
one weekday afternoon,

our voices feeling their way
like explorers in a cave
running their hands along a wall,

the need for talk soon fallen from us
there where the words of a whisper
were like leaves peeling back from the mouth of a spring."

Re-Creation

This is the morning that never was
before, that listens to the robin
listening for the worm, the cedar
choral of the mourning doves;
that takes the path laid down by the slug
beneath the strawberry leaves,
a quivering track like mercury
over the dewfall grass;
this is the day the washing hangs
so full of light and snowy folds
it makes one rippling garment,
a robe tried on by the breeze;
this is the way we take ourselves
on waking into what we are,
the high blue sky without a cloud,
whatever it is that calls to us
out of our own astonishment—
this is the morning.

A Walk Round the Monastery Farm

Gravel and bits of sand in the ruts of the farm road,
every step leaving its little wake of dust,
and the bushes and trees drenched with a shower of birdsong,
the unseen glittering eyes like ripening berries.

Last night over tea in the refectory
the talk contended like the coils of steam
above each glazed white faded china cup,
pure excitement gleaming at the lip.

Today, this confrontation with the world,
oneself alone, oneself against the din
of every single blessed thing alive
rending the silence like the temple curtain.

And still the little cloud of dust behind you
dogging your steps, yet showing you the way.
The road leads up out of the hollow
past an old wagon standing in a field,

its hubs grown rusty as the heads of milo,
the spokewood weathered into cracks and seams.
Up ahead, three pines against the sky
shimmer in the heat as in a dream.

Changing the Flowers

In the newer cemetery, south of town,
the markers barely show above the ground—
the marble bolsters of eternal sleep.
Only the plastic flowers in their urns
keep up the memory across the years
of daisies in a glass beside the bed,
and someone lifted from the pillows there
with someone else's hand beneath his head.

A Reverence

Picking up maple seedpods after a rain,
I am joined by a host of small companions,
a cloud of gnats that follows me around
and stoops only seconds after I do.

They do not help me with the work, of course.
They're more in the nature of an obstacle,
a kind of penance added to the job,
a tiny replica of the Furies

or something medieval like a hair shirt.
Squinting to spot the rain-dark pods in the grass,
I feel them touch down on my tingling back
and hover above the sweat that glistens there,

and for the moment I can imagine
that I'm a monk squinting to thread a needle
in my threadbare cell, a true contemplative,
and these my brothers on the narrow way.

Hoping for Raspberries

They had the right spring,
all right,
those vines
behind the shed,
like strands
of coiling wire
along the ground:
a frosty green,
with thorns
faint red
as the dried blood
of somebody's hands
on them.

The silver-backed leaves
were right
as well,
climbing against
the fence,
with its one rust-
covered, last-year's-
twining-grapevine length
of old
barbed wire,
woven into
the mesh like malice—
hiding

at someone's expense.
And yet
no sign
of a blossom!
I'd fill
the water jug
and soak the ground

a frothy black,
while swel-
tering
beneath the clouds
that rumbled and slid
on by.

One morning I came
to look
again,
and at first glance
I thought
the fruit at last
had come to light,
chill, in the grip
of thorns
(like thimbles
whose wet, pocked sides
kept the tiny seeds
packed tight).

I knelt there trembling
to part
the leaves
and scout out
a pail-
ful of berries,
but what I found
was drops of dew
instead—
like a
mirage in air
receding there, just
ahead.

Stairway

in memory of Bruce Hazen

It is no small thing
to build a stairway
that shall be at once,
ascending or descending,
a lightness underfoot

and so well made
that the stone risers
and treads themselves
(like a fall of water
over the contours

of a shallow ledge,
the whole poise of it
awash in movement,
the light dancing
in place at the edge)

seem to ripple and gleam
as a sign of it.
The glance lingers
on the simple lines,
to take them in.

Breasting that fall
is the flight of mind
that carried out
its first conception
in the sure design.

Ansel Adams: *Aspens, New Mexico, 1958*

Half a dozen slender
bright-sided aspens
set in a clearing
of evening light

(the foreground theirs
in the strip of white
adobe glare
edging their trunks)

before a grove
grown dim and still
as a loft of beams
in a small cathedral.

Something at center
as shy and pale
as the legs of girls
testing the water

steps off,
in that quick gleam,
into absolute rest
and infinite dream.

Lichens

. . . the silver lichen-spots
          rest, star-like, on the stone. . . .
—Ruskin, *Modern Painters*

No sky at evening is more beautiful than this
stray outcrop boulder by the path,
rain-darkened till the lichens show against it
like the stars coming out.

Yet under the telling eye of the microscope,
like footholds leading down a cliff
to the pueblo hid beneath a mesa's rim,
the time-encrusted cracks

reveal other species crowding in and thriving:
the bright orange of *Caloplaca*,
and *Acarospora* in long yellow rows
that started out as gray;

in fact, it would be easy to imagine
beads from necklaces and the small
ears of seed corn scattered in the charcoal
of an abandoned fire,

the housekeeping rubble of an ancient people
deep in dust on a sandstone floor.
The stars themselves, out there in the wheeling dark,
pour their extinguished light.

A Look Around

After supper, wanting a breath of air, we slipped outside
and walked on down the slope where it falls from the cabin.
The ground was soft there with last year's matted grasses;
every few steps some wildflower brought us up,
like coming on a spring still fresheting.
There was the yellow and Argus-eyed
whiskbroom parsley, with leaves like dill,
and the light purple iris,
and the mountain bluebell;
and as we turned back,
a splash of white
bitterroot,
at its
height.

Mid-August in the Mountains

1

Elk slept last night below the cabin,
leaving the grass flattened beneath the pines,
crushed into a redolent green mat.

In the tangled stems, the steaming scat
tells how they rose at daybreak here to dine.
We could have watched them from the cabin.

2

When you knelt in the meadow grass to show me
a dotted gayfeather, its streaming blooms
displayed in lavender against your hand
like pennants at a village festival,
my heart grew light along with yours, we hung
like bees on the lingering thread of scent,
as there in the heat of the late morning sun
I too got down on my knees.

Lightning Bugs

They raise no hair at the back of the neck
like their sizzling namesake. Their light is weak
and intermittent, only resembling
the lightning that's reflected from the clouds
on the horizon, the dry lightning
of a distant storm.

            A lantern, then:
like one of those fixed in the bobbing hat
of a miner working his way to the top,
or a railwayman at his semaphore.
Or it could be someone taking pictures
on the dance floor at a class reunion—
an album's worth of flashes on the dark.

The air along the street is full of them;
each yard is like a drifting constellation.
It's a display that has one end in view,
to single out from kith and kin a mate—
there, at the signal's end, to find one who
has read the impulse right and then returned it
(which is, as I recall, how I found you).

Floating on My Back in the Late Afternoon

Blue above me,
a stretch of blue
clear as a membrane,
touched by the tips
of two white pines.

A cloud starts across,
slipping out from
the upper branches
like shifting snow.
It's full of wet light.

There is a breeze,
I can feel it
on face and hair,
see it in the leaves—
but water alone

has my ear.
It's a gurgling,
an undersound,
like the lapping
of a drain.

In what is left
of the light down here,
the sculling coins
wash up over
the pool's edge,

the children splash
and dive; a ball
floats by. I drift
like someone pointing out
the sky.

From *The Voice We Call Human*, 1991

Next Morning

for Bob and Jane MacLennan

Fresh from the storm, the glistening
tips of the juniper stir in the wind,
stretching out fingers of rainy green
in half-light here at our door.

They resemble our own
sheen and sway, tossed
in the shy gusts of conversation,
and what we hold on by, like them,
is something that leans toward light,
a stem—

         the voice we call human.

A Hot Afternoon with Nothing to Do

A sudden parting of the grass
beneath a pine, the sort of place
a dog works round the field to, given time
and the least scrap of a scent—
but come on our own we find
nothing beyond a few wild irises
and a clearing no larger than a tent.
We have to stoop to enter.
And going down on hands and knees
on a bed of rusting needles
for a closer look at the smoky stems,
we notice a streak of dew
all down one petal, a darkening track
that moves at a snail's pace, as if the flower
had to thaw out to be blue.

Clare's Last Poem

I wrote because it pleased me in sorrow
and when happier it makes me happier
and so I go on.

—John Clare, in a letter, 1832

Long after he went mad, John Clare
kept his hand in out of habit.
He would sit by the hour and stare
at a flower or rabbit

or, as here, at a hazel hedge
where the finch built her nest of moss,
and the wind crept over the sedge,
and one old cow cropped the grass.

Just beyond, he could drink his fill
of the light of spring in the wood.
For a moment the world held almost still,
and the quiet rang in his head.

Antique Wrenhouse

Light as air, the bones
that entered here, the quick
feathered motions, flicker
of wing and tail, bearing
a twig or wisp
of grass, or needle
of pine turned rusty,
to weave into a nest—

and that light air, the song
they ran through here, bubble
of pure quicksilver, piercing
the listener's ear,
is bedded down in silence,
reverberant and clear.

Salt Valley Grange

for Beth Franz

Its meetings are held in a white clapboard church
long abandoned, where the steeple shores up the sky
and the farmers the future has left in the lurch,
facing foreclosure, still hope to get by.

Snowfence in Late April

A stutter of slats
against the sky,
bits of blue in the clouds,
each minute gap
a tap on the telegraph
racing the light on by, the grass
like the emerald seethe and slide
of the tide gone out
in the lobster pots,
the ghost, salt havoc of the drifts
that winnowed them—
one section is on its side.

Vietnam Memorial

for Maureen Franklin

Looking for loved ones in the ranks of names,
the mourners are reflected in the granite
against a drifting accolade of clouds
that brush and tarnish, like breath on a glass.

Pallbearing

We sway catching hold of the handles
while everybody stares,
then lurch away with the coffin,
like helping a drunk downstairs.

Heron Feeding in Rain

Working the shallows of the farm pond,
he wades through algae like a jade-edged mirror.

The light rain preens on the surface;
the heron turns to stone.

He waits for the coil of minnows to come
wreathing its way through the water,

the sullen flash as they turn and fade
like a breath passing into the glass.

He will shatter his own reflection
picking one out as they pass.

Reins

Slowly the rocker, on its curved runner feet,
oak on the oak floor, edges over—
maybe an inch or two a week.

Though not much as far as slippage goes,
the sense of it dizzies her
like a wide turn showering snow,

and so she rises and she moves it back.
Her fingers tighten on the arm-ends
now, as if they gathered slack.

From *To See How It Tallies*, 1995

Driving after Dark

I love the look that stole across your face
as you leaned forward looking up tonight—
spotting Orion and the Pleiades,
lit from within in answer to their light.

Lilac Storm

Over one stretch of wall the lilac buds
swell, loom, lighten as they open out;
the whole bush leans like the glistening flanks
of a thunderhead. And then the downpour
of that giddy scent! As you walk by
it comes to you with a rush of coolness,
an ancient pocket spilling from the brick;
your skin prickles as you encounter it.
No other flower, blooming, looks so wet.
The blossoms drench the air and madden it.

Ritual

Early May, late at night, cat let in.
With both cheeks marks my right leg twice in passing,
with left cheek marks the doorframe leaving kitchen,
with right again the doorframe entering den.
On haunches sits and purrs beside his bowl.

I make small rain fall down of crunchy pellets.
He hunches over, mouths one above white mane.
Purrs while crackling down, purrs swallowing.
His fur in gleams now, like a melting snow.

His fur in gleams, too, in the dark outside,
like snow receding, like the apple bloom
ghostly above his head, or like a beam of moonlight.

(But there is no moon except his round slit eyes
in which those twin horizons stand on end.)

Stands, licks whiskers. Audience at end.

Strayed

From the subscriber, red a heifer, 3
years old; has a small star in her
forehead; is white under her belly,
and a little white to her tail; has a
piece cut off her left ear.—Also,
gone, a young brindle HEIFER,
with a white forehead three years
old, a piece cut straight off the
left ear . . .

—*Ulster County Gazette*, Kingston,
Saturday, January 4, 1800

Though scanter mention is made
of the second heifer that strayed,
I picture her in the cold
(with a forehead three years old
and white as her steaming breath)
wandering with clouds on the heath.

The first gets a bit more press,
with a typical Irish stress
on the doting particular:
a heifer with one small star
on her forehead, and white in her tail,
her underbelly pale.

Which did the owner prefer?
And how old was the rest of her?—
the second heifer, I mean.
And was either one ever seen,
come to her senses at last,
back home in the orphaned grass?

Witness

As I top the rise, there, at the foot of the hill,
a swoop from the wires into the roadside grass,
a tussle and flap of wings, and as I near,
the talons treading out their ancient measure,
the wings arched suddenly in exultation,
the hawk's head slowly turns to me, his eye,
his tilting yellow eye, taking me down and down,
like a wavering stone, into its fathomless waters.

In Minnesota

Through scrub pine, uphill
over a sandy road,
the tires seething beneath us,
my father's friend at the wheel,
the three of us bumpily drove
to Lake Whatever-It-Was.

And pushing out from a slip
into a reedy inlet
and out onto the lake,
we made for the near far side.
The oars thumped on the gunwales,
and the pulled water swirled.

I trailed my hand to the wrist,
catching the swirls like leis.
A loon called from somewhere.
We anchored near a cloud's
reflection on the water,
and the boat lightly swayed.

Passage

Those caterpillars
you brought in
with the parsley and
put in a Mason jar, to
watch them double each day
in girth and length,

gnawing away, dropping
dark green pellets
on the jar's glass
floor, falling asleep,
then waking and
beginning anew, taking on

rippling rolls
of caterpillar fat
till only a single
stalk was left, and one
attached itself to it,
so that the other two

had to make do
with twigs you'd left there
for the pitching of
their metamorphic tents—
by what chemical
intelligence

could they have known
to camouflage the event,
the one a huge jeweled
gall of parsley green,
the others dark brown
as knobs on their twigs?

Having witnessed this
labor, this tortuous
change, what will we feel
at the strange coming heaven
of the broken chrysalis,
the uncramping wings,

black swallowtails
soaring off on their own
out over the yard?
Now, when to think of it
quickens the pulse,
the waiting grows hard.

Reflection

Polishing the copper lining of the doorframe,
I watch the metal pale as it grows clear,
turn almost blond in the October light.

This left-hand strip, its upper half now done,
reflection wading in it like a mirror,
discovers in its depths the polisher

and something more: the neighbors' ash tree,
its leaves like tarnish or a haze of gold.
Some shining dulls, no matter how we rub.

To See How It Tallies

It is a joy of the purest sort,
sitting here in the sun-flooded den
in the not-quite winter light
of the morning before solstice,
the cat asleep in sun on the couch,
one last leaf on the dogwood
bright as a newly struck medallion
beyond the window, where the maple
casts three limb shadows on the glass,
and finding at my foot a feather
on the dark striations of the rug,
a down feather, mouthed by the cat,
dropped and dried into a tiny fern,
to see how it tallies, all of it,
nothing that comes to be or ceases
that is not somewhere accounted for,
its being somehow folded back,
sorted out into the purest joy.

Vigil

All the windows in the house next door
are lit tonight: far into the dark
burn the foursquare blocks of mullioned light.

What they watch for, wait for, I can't tell.
They may not wait at all, any more
than a mirror waits in an empty hall.

And no one looks out, framed in the light
falling gold on the snow. Maybe nothing
keeps watch but window on window.

From *Short Suite*, 1997

Winter Cloud Cover

No stars were out on my walk tonight.
Only a few flakes by the streetlamp,
standing in for the constellations,
fell to improvising on the light.

Diviner

Head tipped back as though it drank,
the meadowlark lets go a song
whose gliding phrases are like water
under the bib's black prongs.

Ripeness Is All, Is All

Five stalks of wild asparagus, in early June,
fan out their feathery green and hint of blue
like a peacock's tail, as if to disparage us
for never before (too late now) having seen.

October Retort

The room is filled with maplespun gold light
from the tree next door, a delicate alchemy
distilled of airy orange and the sky's bright
curve of blue: each leaf lets one hoarded drop fall through.

Crowbar

Cold black as the feathers of a crow's wing
when it was new, grown dull now
except at the end that does the lifting,
where use has worn it smooth as silver—
the shaft's slight curve tapered to a glistening.

Deep Autumn

I slept once in a room that smelled of apples,
on a quilted bed whose clean sheets folded me
like something kept in tissue in a drawer,
a poise of leaves light-heavy in my head,
my dream descending on me in their stead.

First Bite

Not the apple's glint, but the welling core,
the close-packed, dull black seeds.
You cross the yard to the crunch of snow;
the drops on the winch rope freeze.

The Hunter, Home

Behind the neighbors' roof, Orion's down,
all but his head and shoulders,
at two a.m. this mild December night.

Three stories' worth of sloping tiles
drawn up like a comforter!
He reaches, on one elbow, for the light.

From *From the Ground Up*, 2000

At Summer's Height, in Hungary

A bumper crop of cherries bows the trees,
and in Szentendre, north of Budapest,
walking the cobbled back streets, up ahead
we see a man poised on an upper rung
of his ladder, reaching into the leaves
to strip the fruit into a burlap bag.
The ladder stands outside the garden wall,
and leaning and straining over it he keeps
precarious balance, his feet this side,
his head and shoulders and his flashing hands
on that, the very gestures of his work
making him seem to yearn back into Eden,
the old predicament. Once we are by
I cannot keep myself from looking back,
but no sword flares above his heavy sack.

January Primrose

It is the simple pleasures that define
the essence of your nature. So this plant,
brought home through bitter cold to realign
its blossoms by the window where the slant
rays call to it, thrusts out its curled green leaves
around the pure white petals of each bloom,
where at the center throbs a star that cleaves,
in sulphur green, the intermittent gloom,
and each six-pointed star is darkly veined,
a tiny compass orienting here
whose needle never moves and is not strained
by such a vigil on the atmosphere.
The sprinkled plant each morning thrives anew,
its freshened leaves the only sign of you.

First Sighting

The comet stole through darkness to the west
above the last light's transom in the sky,
the rumor of its passage laid to rest
by confirmation of the naked eye.
Between two tall bare trees it pulsed and blurred,
seeming to thrash in place where the debris
(like a waterfall too distant to be heard)
streamed out behind it. And you turned to me
and took my hand in yours and held it tight.
There was no need of words between us then.
Merely by having sought it out in flight
we had received there, like a talisman,
the comet's blessing, and it drew us on,
westward in its wake, toward the horizon.

Reckoning

As for the weighing up of things to date,
so far, and to this point, and as of now,
which is to say (not to prevaricate
or to bend backward in an awkward bow,
but from the waist and forward with some grace
to speak the truth, and see how that may go)
just at this moment, in this very place,
keen as a wet wind that could turn to snow,
at saying's edge, the bursting of joy's grape,
the there-you-have-it there, the tried and true,
the out-of-reach taking a ghostly shape,
the thing that you'd forgotten that you knew—
I'd say that out of all my luck in life
the best stroke's been to have you for my wife.

Back through California

1 Inland at Ojai

Haze in the valley, over the ravine
and back along the ridges toward the sea,
and sound that carries up from a machine
driven to celebrate necessity—
tractor or chug of water like a tug
lurching in spray behind a swell of heat.
And maybe a man with an ice-cold jug
is standing there, the water fierce and sweet . . .

Here on the mountain, not an hour ago,
you picked some lemons back there in the grove,
and the tree stood rippling in its shadow,
like the earth brimming round a spring that dove.
The lemons still were ripening, splashed with green,
their fragrance on your fingers like a sheen.

2 Starting Up the Coast Highway in Mid-Afternoon

Below San Simeon we struck the road
and headed north, the air grown wet and bright,
keeping tall grass and mountains on our right
while on our left a line of breakers showed.
There was a point where yachts and trawlers rode;
a beacon there had shipped its oar of light.
Mist towered out to sea and out of sight.
The salt horizon thinned until it glowed.

We swung back toward the mountains' drift of cloud
and climbed until the view was over cliffs—
cove after cove of waves, a wrinkling snow.
We hardly dared to breathe or speak aloud,
letting our glances over the side like skiffs
abandoned to the rocks there far below.

3 Picking Up the Freeway at Los Baños

Beyond San Luis reservoir, dark trees
take over from the grasses and the hills:
the oranges that in spring are thronged with bees;
almonds, and English walnuts; and the rills
of water that sustain them. The farmer tills
his flat and dusty fields in looping rows;
down corridors the gleam of water spills,
and the wet earth draws sustenance and shows
in leaves and limbs deep-rooted in the flows.
The towns along that stretch lie off the road—
Gustine and Newman, and beyond them, Crows
Landing—arrested by the latter name, I slowed.
The poetry of earth is never dead:
I caught a glimpse of wings far up ahead.

Planting a Dogwood

Tree, we take leave of you; you're on your own.
Put down your taproot with its probing hairs
that sluice the darkness and create unseen
the tree that mirrors you below the ground.
For when we plant a tree, two trees take root:
the one that lifts its leaves into the air,
and the inverted one that cleaves the soil
to find the runnel's sweet, dull silver trace
and spreads not up but down, each drop a leaf
in the eternal blackness of that sky.
The leaves you show uncurl like tiny fists
and bear small button blossoms, greenish white,
that quicken you. Now put your roots down deep;
draw light from shadow, break in on earth's sleep.

Tent Light

The tent is made of two-colored nylon,
yellow and white,
and at the far end there a scribbling fern
seems dipped in light
as it sways in a breeze light as breathing.
Down on one knee
at the entrance, I am the devotee
of what I see:
that almost magic sense of pure translucence,
this petal skin
inside which someone woke this morning, the sky
stretched eyelid-thin,
and saw the light lean down in heaven's stead
a few feet overhead.

From the Ground Up

Here, at the base of the tree, stands water
like a woodland pool, reflecting the lights
and the fine needles of the lower limbs.
This is the part the cat likes best. He leans
in, needle-showering, under the green, sniffs
along those branches for the still, unseen
but redolent whiff of departed birds,
paws at the trunk, then laps up water
with quick back-scoopings of his ladling tongue.
The birds that dot the tree as ornaments
still tempt him, even after all these years,
but he knows better than to strike them now.
They but confirm what he knew anyway—
there *were* birds here, but they have flown away.

Black

Dark, as the inside of a glove is dark,
a space articulate of absence till
the flesh of probing fingers, like a spark,
shall arc across the void of space to fill
and make the leather once more supple; chill,
chill as a chisel's edge in its attack
upon the stone that yields by holding still,
the ring of oil-dull silver and cold black;
slack, like the water of a tide pool, slack
the shallows coiling in the dead of night,
yet reassuring, as the slightest crack
lets in around the door a wedge of light:
implosion's color, in whose wide embrace
there's no exclusion, and no pride of place.

Form

A glass of water on the table,
filled with light from a nearby window—

and though you did not see the light
poured evenly and from all sides

until it fit the glass's contours
and the water's slightest fluctuations

you see the shape the three maintain
and on the table, at the glass's foot,

the light's pale, slightly trembling shadow,
its low reflection like a little moon

or coin of energy plunked down beyond it,
and now your thirst divines this water,

this glass and light, and delves the world—
this much (no more just now) will do.

From *A Far Allegiance*, 2010

Gong

As though I turned over a bright metal shell
that rippled when I lifted it
like the buckle in the middle of a sawblade,
I step behind it. There at the fluted rim
poise the far running fluxions of the sea,
a tide that still resounds far out of sight
in the deep race whose shudder lifts the swell,
whose gray-green distant silence echoes back
to that still moment when the upraised hand,
as from the world's foundations, fell,
and the water shattered on the glassy sand.

Fishheads

As high on the wall of the chicken shed
as he could reach, my grandfather kept
the heads of the catfish that he caught,
each one impaled on a bright, ten-penny nail.
They would face out into the waves of heat
all summer long, each fresh head wearing
a wreath of wrangling flies for several days,
until the skin began to shrink and crack
like leather badly cured, and head by head
a row of skulls appeared.

      When Grandpa sat
on the low-slung bench along the wall
and leaned forward rubbing his hands together,
and then let fly with a dark-as-licorice stream
like a long-held oath from the plug he chewed,
we knew he was about to tell a story,
one that was bound to seem grotesque,
for there, in the glare of white above his head,
a school of weathered skulls adorned the shed.

X-Ray Fitting

I stood on the platform and slipped my feet
into the wide slot that awaited them
in the new Buster Browns. "Have a look, son,"
the salesman said, so I bent over,
and there, through a rubber-bumpered viewer
like the mask of a stereopticon,
my feet were bathed in a green, fluid light.
It was as if they floated up to me
bone by separate bone, two fossil fish
displayed in the stone of the tried-on shoes,
and not the articulate skeleton
of my two-left-footed feet. Ignorant
(as we all were then) of the roentgen's
sleight of hand, at the salesman's kind command
I wriggled my toes, as with a pointer
he showed my mother on the other side
the growing room I had inside this pair.
That was good enough for her. Wrapping up
my old shoes in the new pair's box, he winked
and handed me an unblown-up balloon.
Outside, the leather of my brand-new shoes
gave back the ordinary light, so bright
it made me blink; yet as we walked along
I saw in my mind's eye, as clear as day,
the toes of each foot like a dorsal fin,
the bones within awakened from the stone,
two fossils, in green water, swim away.

The Squarefold

With the first fold you'd make
a long rectangle, headlines facing in,
and that you'd fold in thirds, then tuck,
neat as a pin,

the right end into the left.
Though hardly origami, it was fun,
and something of an art—to craft,
for its short run,

out of the news of the day,
a paper glider you could sail and curve
around a column, or let fly,
if you had the nerve,

in a long looping line
at the top of which it loomed, a bird
reflected in the doorglass, then,
suddenly blurred,

fell stricken to the porch floor.
And if you were any good you did this
on your bike, with a showman's flair
calling to witness

your neighbor customers:
watch this one, how its wide flight will bring it
drifting in, and this, how it sheers,
when I zing it,

at the end, how this one's
back curve lands it smack-dab on the doormat.
One of my earliest passions,
this daily format

(4:00–5:00) of folding,
then packing the bags on the handlebars
and off on my Schwinn like floating
beside the cars

on busy South Street, small
beside the news I carried (polio,
Korea, Bikini Atoll)
in my portfolio.

A Day at the Dentist's

In his office up over the five-and-dime
in a small town just far enough away
I had to take the bus and stay all day,
my father's Uncle Doc would fix my teeth.

I would lean back in the chair and open wide
as he directed, pumped to the height he chose,
feeling his knuckles brush against my nose
as he scraped and cleaned and told me to rinse.

And if he found a cavity (by eye—
he wouldn't use an X-ray), he would fit
a small, old-fashioned, uncascading bit
into his drill, and from over my shoulder,

his monocle mirror's handle on my lip,
would make the spinning wires and pulleys blur
above my head, as the drill dug its spur
deep down into my sweet-tooth enamel.

Then, from the back room, I could hear the swish
of the pestle as he mixed the filling,
the let-up from the tension of the drilling
making me almost drowsy in the chair.

What was that amber jelly on a stick
he'd swab the tooth with, and crimp with cotton?
It lies on my tongue's tip, not forgotten,
still savoring of cinnamon and clove.

Letting me look at his handiwork at last,
he'd ask me to bite softly down on it
and, setting satisfaction's crown on it,
would take me home to lunch on soup and tea.

Produce Wagon

The heat shimmer along our street
one midsummer midafternoon,
and wading up through it a horse's hooves,
and each shoe raising a tongueless bell
that tolled in the neighborhood,
till the driver drew in the reins
and the horse hung its head and stood.

And something in a basket thin
as shavings (blackberries? or a ghost
of the memory of having tasted them?)
passing into my hands as Mother paid,
and the man got up again,
slapping the loop from the reins,
and was off on his trundling wagon.

In the Near Distance

The sound of the freight train rolling by
half a mile away,
each car passing with a thump
over one floating rail,
and up ahead the engine,
brash with its own importance,
hooting around the bend,
the tracks at the end of its light
like the horns of a snail.

Horse Creek Road

(East central Nebraska, September 1884)

1 Hattie Keene

I saw him go by that day—
the next day, it turned out,
after it happened. I was out
in the yard getting in the wash,
and as I took the clothespin
from the corner of a sheet, leaving
a gap like a drape pulled back,
I saw him down there in the road
at the bottom of our lane. He seemed
in no special hurry, just kept along
with his head down, raising his eyes
now and then, but it was George Purnell
and no mistake—fair and small,
a little on the bandy side,
with a ramrod sort of walk—
and his going by like that,
not seeing anything around him,
is what I later called to mind,
hearing what they had found
down there on the Wymer place.
Poor, lovely Mary Wymer,
that darling baby girl of hers,
and Halvorsen, their hired hand,
and Oscar Wymer himself, all
with a bullet through the head,
and kind old Henry Muir, who stayed
with Purnell, dead in the same way.
I had nightmares about them all
for years. And there he was
on the road, calm as you please, the man

responsible: George Purnell.
I keep thinking, if I'd known that day,
I could have got word to someone,
and maybe he wouldn't have got away.

2 Thomas Shadbolt

I never seen the like before, never,
and hope I never do again. Me and Carl
was bringing the cows up over the ridge
from the back pasture, along about noon,
when we seen a man come riding up the road.
It was that deputy fellow, Springer,
and when he seen us up there he reined in,
shouting something we couldn't understand
and motioning back toward the Wymer place
with his free hand, like a man I seen once
in a pantomine. Wellsir, me and Carl
takes right off running across the field,
the goads still in our hands (funny,
we never even noticed till we reached
the fence and had to throw them down, to hold
the wires apart—Carl tearing this big hole
in the shoulder of his shirt, which shows
what a hurry we was in), and then we run
on down that little rise and up the hill
and turned in winded at the Wymers' lane.
The place sets back a hundred yards or so,
and there by the barn door stood the sheriff
and Springer, his horse still shaking its head
and blowing. "We need you boys to help,"
the sheriff said. We stepped inside the barn.
There, slumped over some bales of straw, was Wymer,
with his big shoulders and his barrel chest
resting on the top one, stiff as a board—
they was blood all down one side of his head,
and the bale soaked raspberry red with it.

I took the feet, Springer and Carl the arms,
and we carried him out into the yard
where his old flatbed wagon was pulled up
and hitched to his own horse, a big bay mare,
and laid him on his back, his legs bent up,
arms out, and covered him as best we could
with some empty feed bags. The strangest thing!—
I almost felt like laughing, from the way
he looked there, like a frog gone belly up
beside a lily pad. The sheriff now, he guessed
that Wymer had just brought the horse inside
when Purnell jumped him—one shot, up close,
behind the ear. We was all standing there
by the wagon, and it was awful still,
except for some crows in a tree nearby
making that racket of theirs, which made
the stillness worse. "We better have a look
inside," the sheriff said, and so that's what
we done (I never would have on my own).
Through the kitchen we found the hired man
in a pool of blood on the hallway floor,
and then the woman and the little girl
facing each other where they'd both laid down,
it looked like, to take a nap—all of them
with just the single bullet through the head.
Carl, he was sick behind the kitchen door.
Well, somehow we got them all out of there,
and they was four bodies in the wagonbed
when the sheriff and Springer headed back
to town (Springer on the wagon, driving,
his own horse tied behind) on down the lane
between the rows of wrinkled, unpicked plums,
and then the wagon swung out on the road
and was soon lost from sight. To this day
I never fetch the cows or hear the crows
without that business coming back to me.

3 Dora Clement

I think it was a premonition,
this sort of dream I had.
In it we were coming back from town,
and as we crossed the bridge,
making the planks jump and rattle,
I saw a fox slip down
the edge of that field behind the barn
and, it being sunset,
the light stood like a flame in his brush
just as he disappeared,
and fear took hold of me then, the same
as if I'd seen a ghost.
I saw us pull up in the yard,
a rank smell everywhere,
and my entire flock of pullets
torn to pieces there—
feathers and blood all over the place,
and things completely still.
I was so happy to discover
it had been just a dream
(waking, I ran to the coop to see)
that I ignored its warning
until that day the wagon,
bearing its grisly load,
came creaking by to confirm the meaning
from two farms down the road.

4 Ed Probert

I was sheriff then, and the Wymer case
was the bloodiest one in all my years
with the county. And the most frustrating:
we knew to a certainty who'd done it,
though the why of it was never clear,
and the man himself got clean away.

I won't go into detail as to what
we found there at the Wymers'. A person
just doesn't realize the damage
even a single bullet to the head,
at point-blank range, can do, unless
he sees it, as I had to, for himself.
I think what most upset me was the girl—
she was just a baby—and the fact
that Mary Wymer was far gone with child,
making six dead in all. But at the time
I didn't think of that somehow, the child
buried unborn inside its mother's body.

Here's what took place, as near as we could tell:
Purnell had living with him, on his farm,
an old bachelor friend named Henry Muir,
and what set him off, it seems, was a game
of cricket—*cricket*, of all things!—
over at Squint Hopkins'. Now both Purnell
and Wymer (and maybe old Muir as well)
had come from England, and they missed the game,
so they'd meet with others for a friendly match—
only this time there was an argument.
Hopkins says Purnell got awfully mad—
he thinks, maybe, because old Muir had been
paying Sarah Byrne too much attention.
George was soft on Sarah, everybody
knew it, and it seemed to aggravate him.
It might have been a quarrel over land,
as far as that goes, or some money Muir
had promised and not paid him; anyway,
that night, when Muir turned in, Purnell shot him,
once, in the back of the head. (We found
the bullet in the bedroom wall.) Next day,
early, Halvorsen, the Dane hired man,
dropped by to ask if he could talk to Muir

(at any rate, that's what we figure).
Parnell made something up to put him off,
then likely got to thinking that the Dane
somehow would put two and two together,
so sometime after lunch he crossed the fields
(they're neighboring farms) to the Wymer place.
He may have had words with Halvorsen
at the kitchen table (a broken mug
and coffeesplash were lying on the floor);
anyway, as the Dane went to his room
Purnell followed down the hall and shot him
from behind, then ran on down the hall
and murdered Mary and the little girl
as they lay sleeping in her bed (again
leaving his signature, one bullet each
in the back of the head). My God, the mess!
Wymer himself had spent the day in town,
and that bowlegged little S.O.B.
must have hid in the barn till he drove in
and jumped him just as soon as he got down.
We're not sure if Purnell stayed there that night
or went back home. Next day, by late morning,
he was on the road. Walking, for some reason,
though there wasn't a thing wrong with his horse—
he'd left it pastured back at his place.
Maybe he thought he'd be conspicuous
pelting away on horseback; out here, though,
a man on foot's more likely to be noticed.
Then again, maybe he didn't think at all.
I've never known what could possess a man
to do a thing like murder on that scale.
I don't expect I ever will.

5 Sarah Byrne

Oh yes, I was sweet on George,
but not enough to marry.
There were times when he frightened me.

He had the darkest blue eyes
I ever saw, the color
of a fully ripe blueberry,

dark as the anchor on his arm
(back home once, drunk on perry,
he'd gotten it tattooed,

he said, and here on the prairie,
where the grass was more like the sea
than the sea, it steadied him

whenever he longed for home).
I loved the name he gave me then:
I was his "darlin' Sary."

6 C. B. Sears

Yessir, they tell me the man I saw's
the very one. Kept pacing up and down
the platform; caught the 8:15.
Wearing a farmhand's pants and fancy shirt
he was (a getup, I understand,
he'd borrowed off two of the dead men).
I closed the door behind him with a click,
and the train lurched and started down the track.

Certificate

The thick, cream-colored paper, stiff with age,
is conjured from its uncapped mailing tube.
My friend unrolls it on the tablecloth
like a disused drumhead; one curling end
keeps scrolling up on him until we help.
We anchor its four corners with the salt
and pepper, and with a pair of ashtrays,
and then lean over, our pointing fingers
ready.

     A relic of his father's past,
it's official paper, attesting trove,
witness (like the godhead, three-in-one)
to a birth, baptism, and confirmation:
geboren 1898 in some
far Ukrainian hamlet that to us,
in its straight-up-and-down old German script,
now reads as Anywhere You Damn Well Please:
his father's people having been among
the second wave of Germans settled there
after the lead of Catherine the Great
a century before, whose policies
still drew and prospered them; and then confirmed,
according to this, in 1913,
the young man who would read theology
(which, in this country, he would put to use,
a fierce agnostic, to refute the claims
of all believers, and especially
the Armageddon crowd who had the world's
end worked out to the millisecond—
who fondly quoted St. Luke's caveat,
"For the Son of Man cometh at an hour
when ye think not," like the very Devil

quoting scripture to his devious ends):
but that would all come later, with the years
of showing horses at the county fairs,
at the fallen, bitter end of his career.
Here on this paper now he is fifteen
and foreign-Ukrainian, yet to leave
his family and their calculations for him,
the cold love that trained him for a pastor
and consigned him to bringing in the sheaves—
to take his passage for America
and be the son that every family grieves.

We hover thus over his story here—
or its beginnings. The certificate
takes all our breath away, its borders dressed
with tabs like an entablature of stone,
making the document look almost like
an altar front or window of stained glass:
there are panels bearing Bible quotes,
and the gold leaf backgrounds of medallions
framing the icons of their images
(grapeleaf and cluster, chalice, lamb, and crown),
and swags of grapevine, leaf, and tendril
worked round and in among familiar scenes
from Christ's own ministry. Incredible
the soft white chalky blues, the iodine
of sash and snow-white of a sleeve, the whole
strict harmony of gesture here, and background,
and with what certainty the Edward Staib
mentioned but once here (but that once for good)
turned from all the certainties around him.

The Carny Circuit

for Adam Staib

1 Keeping the Horses

The boy had been alone for fifteen days
before the thought occurred to him: this time
maybe the old man wasn't coming back
at all. It was just him and the horses,
feeding their way around the tether-stakes
in a good bit of meadow by the road,
the boy sleeping out with them at night
upon the ground (the nights not yet grown cold),
by daylight watching over them until
he half suspected when he talked to them
they were about to answer—those great eyes,
the telltale shivers in the flank and haunch.
Even the horses had been feeling it,
the small uneasiness that moved inside him.
He brushed them down, went to fetch water
up from the creek a hundred yards away;
hauling it back, he heard the water sway
and lap against the bucket at his side.
A car went by from the farm down the road.
He waved, and the driver waved, and the dust
swept out and made a tunnel in the air—
a tunnel that would suddenly collapse.
And he thought of his mother through the years
trying to glimpse, like that, his father's quick,
authoritative passage through their lives.
He would be drinking now, talking about his plans
with someone that he'd met in some dark bar,
the truck and van parked outside, the dust
of this same road on top of other dust

from all the roads they'd driven down that year,
following the circuit of the county fairs
with a ramshackle carnival, the horses
sometimes performing in a lot out back
and sometimes to a grandstand audience.
Near towns down those back roads, more and more of late,
they'd pull off onto the grassy shoulder
by a gate that led into a pasture,
backing the animals down the splintered ramp,
his father fashioning a long rope halter
to lead one horse around with at a time
and give the local kids a ride. It cost
two bits some days, on other days a dime,
the difference being what the old man lacked
by way of change to jangle in his jeans.
There was never any money for the boy;
the old man never thought that anyone
had needs except himself. And they were poor,
God, but they were poor! Many a time
they'd lifted out the seat up in the cab,
just to scrounge around for coins: in fun
they called it "going to the bank." (He thought
of the old man, frantic for money now,
lying across the pitted running board,
his long legs out at angles in the street
like toppled stilts beside the worn-out seat,
hoping to pick up on the littered floor
a beer or two in change . . .)

                The sun had dipped
into the lower branches of the cottonwood
down by the creek. Every day now that moment came
a little sooner, and the boy saw how
the grass went deep and almost wet with light
at that lower angle. He walked back down
toward the stand of trees for some kindling wood.

One thing that you could say for the old man:
there was always plenty of food in cans
for cooking over a fire; as for talk,
they'd never come close to running out of that.
Still, with him gone he didn't miss the talk.
It was good to have the outdoors to himself,
or the feeling of that, the horses there
stirring and nickering, snuffling in the dark
beyond the fire, the stars darting their glints
far back down to him from a wet black sky.
The first few days it seemed to him as if
the old man was still around, but lately
he'd noticed he'd begun to let things go,
begun to grow wild along with the horses.
There were times he wished he could run like them,
the ground reverberating under him,
nothing between him and the open sky
but his shadow floating out over the grass . . .

He rummaged in the canvas knapsack bottom
for the opener. For supper he'd have beans,
cooked in a shallow pan until the bubbles
snapped in the juice like lava on the run—
nothing better, sopped with a hunk of bread.
He thought he'd move the tether-stakes tonight;
then maybe afterwards he'd leave the fire
and walk down by the bridge to listen
to the water gurgling in its glimmering banks.
One of these nights the old man would be back,
and more and more his thoughts were fixed on that.
For several days he'd had a kind of dream
shaping inside his head, a dream in which
he saw himself eyeing his father there
at the firelight's edge—the boy angry
at being left alone to watch the horses,
and running against the old man with his fists.
It was a dream he willed and yet could not

control: always his father in the dream
would catch his wrists and wrap him in his arms,
and the boy, sobbing, had to catch his breath.
It was only a dream—no use to him.
He knew tomorrow, next day, sometime soon,
he'd hear the truck come rattling up the road,
just in time for supper, probably,
the old man getting out and glad to see him,
wiping his mouth on the back of his hand
in that absentminded gesture of his,
as casual as if he had been gone
an hour or two at most, and then he'd say,
"How's my boy?" and ask about the horses.

2 The Lookout

It was getting late in the afternoon
when we started up the long sandy lane
toward a farm set back in the hills, the tin
shimmer of its roof like a mirage.
I had seen the flash of it, like water,
from the road a good half mile beyond
while the old man was cussing out the pickup,
the radiator hissing and blowing steam,
the horses shifting nervously in the van.
Bridling them, we got them down and set off,
hoping to stable them and spend the night—
the old man up ahead with Queenie,
me following behind with Bess. It was hot,
even for the end of August, and tired
and thirsty and out of sorts as we were,
I could understand the old man muttering
a blue streak under his breath. Somewhere east
of Limon, expected the next day
to show up in Denver with the horses
and work a carnival at a county fair,
here we were, say, seventy miles away.

All I could hear as we plodded up the lane,
beside the *chish chish* of the hooves in sand,
was the steady gasp of the old man's cussing.
But when we came up over the last rise
and saw the place, that silenced him for once,
and both of us let the reins hang slack,
taken aback for a moment there:
the L-shaped house of weathered, graying boards,
a few chickens pecking round the yard,
and by the barn out back a cottonwood,
with running water purling underneath
the rustle of its leaves. As we drew up
a man came out onto the shaded porch,
making a visor of one lifted hand
against the glare we stood in, the other
tucked into the bib of his overalls.
The horses stamped and nodded at their bridles,
their heads sawing up and down like oil pumps,
the man himself nodding at intervals
in answer to something the old man said.
And as they talked I saw, chalk-white behind
the doorscreen, there for a moment and gone
like a ghost, the slack features of a face
almost a boy's, on the body of a man.
"He says it's all right for us to stay,"
I heard the old man saying, swinging round
with Queenie and heading for the barn,
and swinging in behind with Bess, I took
one quick last look back over my shoulder
and thought I saw, just for a moment there,
that face again around a curtain's edge
in the small front window.

               They called him "Reef"—
I don't know why. He was simple-minded,
the kind that can't talk, really, but they try,

working their jaws round what they mean to say
as if they chewed it, or as if they blew
the rainbow bubble of each soapy word
and saw it stretch and shine and break
to kingdom come, the slick and slobber of it
on their lips. It made you sad to see it.
He was enormous, with big, rounded shoulders,
and yet not fat: there was a kind of tautness
to his body. He wore a crew cut and a kid's
expression on his face. He seemed a kid.
That night at supper he sat apart from us
at a bread board pulled out from the counter
for him, lifting huge forkfuls to his mouth,
sucking and smacking at his food. A hum
of pleasure came thrumming from where he sat
tipped forward on a tall round kitchen stool.
And when his plate was empty he would bang
it with his fork, and a big quiet woman
at the end of the table would get up
and fetch the plate and fill it at the stove
and then return it to him, and he'd dive
back in, smacking and humming, spilling some
over onto the bread board and the floor.
God, he could shovel it in! The woman
must have got in her exercise that way,
rising to take his plate and fill it up
and hand it back again. Besides herself
there were four of us at the table,
seated around on two low wooden benches:
the man on one side with his hired hand,
a guy named Bud, me and the old man
heads over our food on the other side.
Reef finished up and sat there fidgeting,
rocking back and forth on the creaking stool,
both hands on its rim between his legs
like a rider being bucked up on the reins,

his left foot on the floor as though he stood
in the near-side stirrup. And all the while
he kept on staring at me, making me
uncomfortable, and yet somehow that look
singled me out as if he'd leaned and whispered
a secret in my ear.

          About an hour
after supper, someone pulled up outside
and came on in, not bothering to knock—
a man in one of those cowboy hats
of gappy straw that looked like wickerwork,
a peacock feather's eye stuck in its band.
Soon he was followed by a couple more,
and then by maybe half a dozen others
all at once, talking a mile a minute.
A pair of folding tables was brought out,
and several packs of cards, and just like that
two games of five-card draw were underway.
There was also a game called "Texas Charley,"
with rows of punch holes on a heavy lapboard.
It cost you a dollar to try your hand
but you got back five on a winning number.
I heard the man tell Reef to go on down
and keep an eye out for the sheriff;
holding him by the shoulders, he said it
several times to be sure he understood.
Reef nodded once and then went out the door,
but peered back in through the sagging doorscreen
as if to remind me of when I'd seen him first
that afternoon. I thought of following,
but something held me back, and I went out
to the kitchen. Above the sink a light
was on, and on the stool at the bread board
the woman sat at her embroidery,
working a violet thread through the cloth,

her fingers forming, on the hoop of white,
one of the petals of a flower. She smiled
at me, then bent to her work again, as if,
from years of tending Reef, she'd gotten used
to saying next to nothing.

                The front room
was full of the smoke of the men's cigars
when I returned. Chewing his underlip,
the way he always did when concentrating,
the old man sat there studying his hand.
He never even saw me standing there—
none of the men did. It was almost still
in the narrow room: only the click
of the chips piling up in little mounds
to raise the small-stakes ante, the voices
moving clockwise as the bets went round,
and the smacking down on a tabletop
of a folded hand. There was nothing,
absolutely nothing, for me there.

It was like escaping to slip outside
into the smell of sage, beneath the stars!
Out in the pitch-black barn I ran one hand
along the side of an empty stall,
feeling for a bucket that I'd left there,
a heavy one of wood with metal bands.
Just after we arrived I'd used it
to water the horses from the stream nearby.
The bucket was still damp around the rim
when my fingers found it in the darkness,
and somehow touching it made visible
the faintest light there, like drifting dust,
that must have entered from a chink somewhere.
The handle dug in as I lifted it.
I stepped out through the barn door with it
and crossed a strip, about a stone's throw wide,

of hip-high weeds that switched against the sides—
there was a little sandy path there,
and just enough light for me to pick my way.
As I came up to the cottonwood
I could hear, above the swirl of water,
the faint and steady patter of the leaves,
and the current showed in occasional glints.
Using the bucket as a kind of campstool,
I sat and watched the water gliding by.
After a while I stood and stretched, then kneeled
and dropped the bucket in. The current caught
and dragged it under. Hauling it up,
I felt it slosh, and spilled some over the side,
and the smell of the water-freshened staves
came to my nostrils. But when I turned
to head back up the path, I felt a chill
at the back of my neck, and a lurch
in the stomach that made me catch my breath,
and knew at once that someone was standing there
watching me in the dark. Trying to run
bowed over with the bucket at my side,
I slopped the water, crooking my neck
to look back as I went, and then I turned
and froze there in my tracks: dead ahead,
not fifteen feet away, was a figure
grainy and dim as a ghost, and I lost
my grip on the handle.

                    The bucket lay
over on its side, the thin sluice at its lip
now slowing to a trickle as it ran.
It was Reef—Reef who had startled me.
I think I knew that even at the time,
as I felt the metal handle leave my hand
with the strange, heavy lightness of a dream.
It was only Reef. I watched him come up,

take the bucket, and head down to the stream,
the weeds switching against him as he went,
and fill it kneeling there in one long pull
against the current, and haul it dripping
back to me. Then, holding it by one hand
and pointing at it with the other, he tried
to make me understand—something about
the water—and motioned me close to see.
And there, like lights on a river, I saw
the quivering reflection of the stars
on the bobbing surface. He would let it still,
then tip the bucket slightly up again
and make them run, and then he'd laugh out loud.
It seemed great fun to him. I don't know
how long we stood like that, Reef laughing
and talking his babble over the stars.
But when I told him that he'd better go—
I didn't want him to be caught out there
when the man thought that he'd be down the lane
watching for the sheriff—he took me
by the arm and squeezed it, and looked me
in the eye, then nodded and turned away.
He went off round the corner of the house.
I picked up the bucket where he'd set it,
then watered the horses and went inside.
The poker was still going strong. The woman
showed me to a corner of the pantry,
and I put down my bedroll and turned in.

In the morning you couldn't say a thing
to the old man, and that meant that he'd lost.
We ate a standup breakfast and went out
and bridled the horses, then started
down the lane. At the rise I turned and waved,
hoping that Reef might be there at the window.
I couldn't tell if he waved back at me.

Across the Sandhills

Sometimes for days the only travelers
for miles around
are things that do not keep to the ground:
cloud shadows, a hawk on the wing,
wind in the grass, the telephone wires
rising and plummeting.

A Freshening

Like a hose turned on
at the side of the house,
its water burbling and chuckling
off into the grass
at the other end,
making a pulse and flash
in the gathering darkness,

the cicadas begin
as at a signal,
drawn out en masse
not in a trickle but a full-
throated pouring out,
sandy as from a spring—
a three-minute song like a shout.

Woman Feeding Chickens

Her hand is at the feedbag at her waist,
sunk to the wrist in the rustling grain
that nuzzles her fingertips when laced
around a sifting handful. It's like rain,
like cupping water in your hand, she thinks,
the cracks between the fingers like a sieve,
except that less escapes you through the chinks
when handling grain. She likes to feel it give
beneath her hand's slow plummet, and the smell,
so rich a fragrance she has never quite
got used to it, under the seeming spell
of the charm of the commonplace. The white
hens bunch and strut, heads cocked, with tilted eyes,
till her hand sweeps out and the small grain flies.

Upriver

(. . . the Missouri)

Think of the water glimpsed through trees from a bluff,
a glint that carries like the far-reflected snow
in the mountains, the light on a barge's prow,
the years floating by full-laden from upstream:
trappers and traders in fur, the promised land
beyond the booming arc of Rainbow Falls, the water
leading by ladder stages to the weirs
of beaver, buffalo darkening the grass
like the grazing shadows of clouds; round many a bend
a steamboat wreck still founders, gone under again in silt;
along the coast of the abandoned forts,
a glittering desolation of one-horse towns,
the brittle thunder of cracking ice, and a chilling ring
like the cold drawn steel of sabers: Fort Benton in ruins,
and Fort Union where the smallpox came, leaving
its deadpan traces in Larpenteur's account;
the lodgefires dead and scattered through the pages
of the treaties, the women and children's ghosts
(Cree and Blackfoot, Mandan, Otoe, Sioux)
like wind on the water, the air round the string of a bow.

Laid Down at Mesa Verde

Stoneblade knives, awls and scrapers of bone;
small mortars for grinding paint,
their basins stained with the earthen ends of the rainbow;
the luminous pottery in geometric patterns,
with now and then a carousel of animals—
turtles, toads, or deer—around the rim of a jar,
or a delicate bird stepping out
in a shoal of glints at the bottom of a bowl;
the kiva storage jars, with ripple finish;
specimens of corn, beans, and squash,
and stone metates and manos for making meal;
not much in the way of jewelry
but a cache of shells, stashed in a trader's bag
brought all the way from the Pacific,
a necklace of two strands made out of them,
and some pieces of turquoise and jet;
inside the tower at Cliff Palace,
red ocher paintings round the upper walls;
the houses built back into the cave
right up to the sandstone overhang,
like the empty clay nests of swallows;
and suddenly, there they are,
swallows dipping and riding the draft
to disappear through a crack overhead,
their twitter sounding out a loft,
a vault locked into the ceiling:
a muffled call like the cries of the People
from deep in the rock.

West of Vegas

1 Red Rock Canyon

Sagebrush and joshua
establish the range of green;
the sky counsels lightly
and moves on.

Like a cloud over a peak,
light glints from a rock
and is gone.

Everything rides on a glance
as quick as a tongue.

The hike to the springs,
the blacktop spur
to Lost Creek Canyon,

the savor of water
in every place name:
oh, kneel and drink
in the desolation.

2 Mt. Charleston

There, in the break ahead,
snow mist over the valley;
suddenly desert scrub
is pine and cedar.

The gray stone bed
of Deer Creek scrabbles down
from a source in the clouds.

It goes to your head,
this lighter air, this tick of flurries.

The pull of the grade
whines in the engine;
cliffs tower above pines.

The air outside
is wet and gray, a few
large flakes swirl lazily
as we enter the lodge.

Under Magnification

I stoop to the telescope as if leaning in
under stone at the mouth of a cave
and enter the passage of the barrel,
emerging in a vault of stars
roofed over by the dark,
and there it is: Praesepe,
the beehive cluster, in a glister
of rays like iridescent wings,

the gleam I saw once in the tomb at Mycenae—
the stone hive towering inside
the grassy hill, and a shaft of light
trickling over the sill
of a sky-blue aperture where, coursing
in their shimmering orbits,
bees hovered in the air above us
like the faint humming of the spheres.

The Water Meadows, Winchester

The air above the almshouse all atwitter
where the swallows dipped and soared,

and through the doorway, in the empty courtyard,
the light let go and poured

a gold that rippled through the one tree's leaves
like coins that somehow rustled.

Further on, a man fly-fished for grayling
where the water gurgle tussled

with an elm tree's roots at a bend in the stream,
the flash and turn like a scythe,

and there on the far side once went poor John Keats,
gleaning his harvest tithe.

Near Dorchester, in Dorset, from the Train

We'd slowly wound southeastward out of Bath
until we caught the milk run toward day's end.

Beyond one little station was a man
who stopped his rake to lean upon its end.

And I remember once beside the tracks
a tiny shack where sidings made an end.

And then a field below a wooded hill
where light fell and a fox fur stood on end.

At dusk we stretched and then got down our grips
and stood them on the platform, end to end.

O'Keeffe's *Barn with Snow*

Start with the clean foundation, blocks of stone,
here on the right forming an underwall
where the foreground slopes suddenly away,
the threshold and the anchor of the scene.
Two drifted sills relieve the wash of grays
that is the barn's near wall, and up above,
but lightly dusted underneath the eaves,
a mow gives on a grainy darkness lit
by shades of brown ascending from within.
The snow defines the sharp edge of the roof.
The back, abutting section, of light gray,
is viewed end-on. Its sills, too, are drifted,
its roof's deep well of shadow overhung
with a red cast reflected from the shed
that stands before it, and the near wall's eaves,
from end to end, with that same red are strung.
Rectangle, pentagram, off-center square,
the shapes conjoin: what's abstract here is real.
Only the near wall's roofline is obscure,
its height of snow touching the cloud above
and melting into it, making one squint
to make it out there, barely, on the left,
the sky's low radiance now nearly one
with the white hush that has descended here.

From *The Sledders,* 2016

Simple Gesture

The child you were at one year reaches out,
right hand a blur, to touch a poppy bud.
The world in black and white's not yet in focus,
but on your left, about at shoulder height,
one poppy's satin crepe flares out in red.
The sunlight sprawls in long grass at your feet,
paying its daily homage, and one shaft
plays with the light breeze in your light brown hair.
So here you are, fingers of your left hand
curled delicately under round a shadow,
your cotton dress and collar poised with you
at the beginning of another day—
your spirit filled with wonder at the morning,
this simple gesture all there is to say.

Discovering Gravity

I'm three years old as memory begins:
Shreveport, Louisiana is the scene:
I'm in my stroller at the grocery store
when Mother wheels me past a row of bins
and round the corner, where the gaps between
the glass jars towering above the floor
let in a broad sweep of fluorescent light:
the beets they house are ruby red and bright.

Lacking a grasp of physics, I reach out,
plucking a jar that rests at just my height;
slowly the pyramid of glass gives way,
then quickly caves and shatters. Fear and delight
fill me at once; Mother, however, shouts
my first and middle names in her dismay.

The Sledders

A little down the street from where we sat
sipping coffee and eating chocolate cake
(and here the years flew by in nothing flat,
so that I had to do a double take
to take it in, that painting on the wall
in which three boys on sleds sped down the hill
through lucid half-light, making me recall
my own rough-mittened fingers and the chill
of those long-vanished winter afternoons,
their one-time peer who only watched them now
in this milieu of cups and clinking spoons,
the limbs above the street picked out in snow
as if pure line were all the light discerned),
my sweat (like theirs) once froze until it burned.

In Possession

Something almost Flemish about that water,
a golden brown but clear into its depths,
the plank-ends of the dock a fading gray
beside it, and a boat moored at the end;
something, it seems to me in looking back,
about a murky bullhead on a stringer,
one of those rope ones you can hardly see,
so that the fish appeared to scull in place;
something (the details start to widen now)
about white wooden clapboards on the side
of that inn or tavern where my dad had stopped,
a neon beer sign staring out through glass—
late in the afternoon, I drinking deep
of everything I saw, now mine to keep.

Toward Evening

On Shakespeare's birthday the apple blossoms burst
open like candles on our ancient tree.
It was their white that caught my eye at first,
full of a waxy light that came to be
shell pink or coral when it reached the edge
of every petal shivering in the breeze,
as if that touch of color were the verge
between the snows and the marauding bees.
And then the light began to dim. Each bloom,
steeped in translucence like a bank of snow
melting from underneath, grew pale in gloom,
then disappeared, with nowhere it could go.
At first I thought, There's nothing else to see.
Then a faint shimmer hinted at the tree.

Therefore

let us, love, be ourselves, and nothing less;
let that be adequate to all occasions.
And let the flecks of gold in your brown eyes
bespeak the unplumbed riches of your soul.
Let them bring you the world in soft surprise,
that everywhere you look may recreate
the brimming wonder of a learning child.
Let wrath be turned back by your answer mild,
and every supplication find a voice
to stutter its petition in your heart,
and "Yes!" resound as love's most willing choice.
May everything you love be kind to you,
and may these words eschew the taciturn
to let you know with what deep love I burn.

Laughter

(on a photograph by William Carter)

His hands are almost folded in his lap
as if in reverence, and yet his eyes
sparkle behind his glasses' heavy lenses,
his grin extends from untrimmed ear to ear.
She in turn leans in a little toward him,
one of her arms eclipsing one of his,
her downtilted face spread out in laughter
as though his wry wit had just registered.
This moment is a kind of bond between them,
a secret that they share, a setting out,
a lightening of their common human burden,
and every gnarled or wrinkled sign of age,
and every haberdasher's oddment here,
claims its own share in their good time together.

Similitude

Like Sappho's apple
at the top of the tree,
I find this one
in trimming back
a branch—as with
her pickers, not one
I missed but one
I couldn't reach
(for "pickers" read
"suitors")—fully ripe
and trembling, slightly
astir on its stem,
then rocking back to
stillness, just like them.

For Instance

I learned a prairie secret: take the numbing
distance in small doses and gorge on the
little details that beckon.

—William Least Heat-Moon, *PrairyErth*

Consider these, in blossom by the road:
some poppy mallows, several clumps of them
bent over in the wind on hairy stems
as if their pollen were a heavy load—
sprung overnight where no one saw them sowed,
their petals fluttering like sails they trim,
each slowly stands up on its stem again
from paying its obeisance as it bowed.
Some slight subservience becomes the proud.
And when the wind slacks and the sky grows dim
and a chill moment passes over them
as the mallows feel the shadow of a cloud,
they place their faith in the return of light:
it will come back, grown warm again, and bright.

Watching You Open Your New, Many-Hued Umbrella

With a double flick
of a button, quick
as a blink of the eye,
an imitation sky
unfurls beyond your fist,
like sunlight through a mist
gilding a weathervane
after a pouring rain.

This is a rainbow set
to keep you from the wet,
that even has the power
to dredge up from a shower
(making the colors sing)
the spectrum's sundering.

The Earth Coming Green Again

Uncollected Poems

The Earth Coming Green Again

Here, at the roots of the grass,
earth on its long axis
turns to us as it was,

as a flame leans out and catches
a climbing hold on each blade
and the yard is laid in swatches

of ashy, flickering green.
O delicate shining!
I warm to you as a sign

that something was coming to pass
out here in cold and darkness,
with the sun at its southernmost,

and now I know what it was:
desire completing its course
in every natural crevice

until the whole sky was spanned
with energy to burn
and, taking its own sweet time,

swung home like a compass hand.

A Counterpoise

The garden in July
starts suddenly to lean
this way and that, under green.
The plot's gone all awry.

The dill has grown so tall
it looks us in the eye
like a peacock's tail let fly,
and the impending ball

at the green onion's tip,
as if about to fall
or be toppled after all,
has spun off at the lip

of balance, in the nick
of time, now letting rip
with these little fingertip-
size blossoms. There's a rick

of them, arrayed like stars
around a center, thick
as thieves, awning-striped and quick
with seed. While glinting jars

await the strutting dill,
between the rows, like scars,
the rut fills in as far as
the light can sprawl or spill.

The Sparrow's Way

His song makes free
with reticence.
It says, Let go, let go.
Then, as if to show
me, he alights from the fence,
light edging his wings,
and pecks in the dirt,
puffs out his feathers,
hops and gapes. His eyes
are full of what he knows,
and when he flies back
up to his perch,
breaking the plane
of the sun again
like a catch in the breath,
his shadow skims
the cold, cold ground
and comes to him.

Dakota Burial

*(on a photograph of a Native American gravesite
by David Barry, taken in the 1870s)*

There: in the trees
at the top of the draw
(they look like hackberries,
budded, the ground below
dark as after a thaw,
a few stray wildflowers
studding the grass),
the two bodies lie
shrouded like lowered sails,
angled to the hills beyond
as if they rode on skiffs
tossing on either side
of a wave. The grass
behind them, flecked with sun,
is like a slick of foam.
They turn with the tide for home.

Househunting

We went through a bedroom, then down a flight
of three short steps into the humid air
of a greenhouse the man had added on
because his first wife had ordered orchids
and had no place for them to winter over.
She was long since dead, but he had come to find
a consolation in the flowers. Married
a second time, he brought the new wife here
to share her bed, beyond which, late at night,
the blossoms stirred like the exhalations
of a ghostly lover. Now he was selling
the place—at a reasonable price,
considering he figured in the greenhouse.
The orchids he couldn't bear to part with.

"I've got about four thousand dollars' worth
all told—a considerable investment.
But more than that, I'm fascinated by them.
Some grow in the ground, you know, from bulbs;
others are epiphytes and feed on air.
Or rather, their roots do: they're specially
adapted, some with a corklike covering
to draw the moisture from the air around them.
I've limited myself primarily
to three: *Phalaenopsis, Cattleya, Vanda*.
The *Vanda* is that blue one over there.
There in the corner, that's *Cattleya*,
the big white one. The *Phalaenopsis*
are these right here: they're my special favorites.
They grow on slopes in the Himalayas."

My gaze roamed on its own around the room,
picking out species that he hadn't mentioned.
On a long table there in front of us

stood maybe twenty plants, each with its own
trellis of strings to hold it in its climb,
each bloom with a wide, uplifted face
like a calf or a nun in a wimple.
Their colors were lilac, green, and salmon,
overlaid with the faintest cast of white:
if they looked like nuns, they were giddy nuns,
lightheaded from a long and shriving fast.

"I don't know what it is about these flowers—
you can almost become obsessed by them.
It may be the constant care that is required
to grow them artificially:
a hardly varying environment,
just the right touch of dampness in the air,
the light at a slant on them, and not direct;
in fact, I built those hatches up above
just so the right amount could be let in.
See that hole? I take this pole and hook it
in, like this, and pull it down like a trapdoor.
Before, with only the bare glass roof,
a flood of light came pouring down through it,
far too much for the flowers to thrive on.
Now, it's like a window I can open
on the sky, and let in what they need.
I've had the hatches in for ten years now.
Before that, and before I put the lights in
so I could come out here to work at night
(or leave them on on a dark rainy day),
Adys, that's my first wife, used to like
to come here evenings, and in the half-light
we'd fuss around the orchids, and we'd talk.
One night we talked about the gatherers,
the foragers who brought the rhododendrons
back to England to be bred by Rothschild,
and the first gleaners of the *Phalaenopsis*,

climbing a streamside in a rocky gorge
where the flowers gazed up through the drifting spray,
the sun above them bright on the clouds and snow
of the mountains. It's a feeling for that,
perhaps, that a person gets caught up in—
a kind of reverence for the faraway."

He paused, then took a few uncertain steps
in the direction of the door, abashed
at having opened up to strangers.

"I don't mean to make it sound romantic;
of course it's mostly been a lot of work.
The flowers themselves are the compensation.
Nothing comes up to them—not even winning,
as these often have at flower shows.
I tell you, one of the prettiest sights
I ever saw was when my *Vanda* took
first prize in an open competition—
I don't mean your ordinary ribbon
but that watered-silk-like stuff, a rippled blue
draped over the pot beneath the blossom,
the flower a richer and deeper blue.
Really, a person only understands
if he or she's involved with growing them.
Of course you wouldn't have to use the greenhouse
for raising flowers: it could be done over
into a rec room, or maybe a den.
I sure will miss it when we sell the place!
I'll have to fix up something when we move."

In Blowing Snow

Where the exit was
I couldn't tell exactly—
guessing gave me pause.

As if in a cloud
it was white all around me,
a raw cotton shroud.

There! In foggy snow
the turn-off sign showed ghostly.
I began to slow.

What if I missed it?
I would drive to the next one,
the windshield misted,

skid off-road perhaps,
be surprised by a gully,
feel the white collapse.

Staking everything
on my sense of where it was,
by intuiting

I held to that curve
successfully—not once
did I have to swerve,

nor once consider
how thin was the wire I crossed.
The wind, still bitter,

kept icing the glass,
kept it up all the way home.
But it let me pass.

The Hadderways

Everyone knew them—and nobody did.
They had a place out south of town a ways,
the little house penned on the east and west
by all the barns and sheds in which they kept
the oddments from the farms that came their way
by swap or sale, or in default of loans:
mint-condition antique phaetons
among worn harrow rigs and rusty scythes.
One outbuilding held beneath its rafters
a kind of Hall of Fame of radios,
consoles and portables, and several crystal sets.
The house itself was a No-Woman's-Land;
dark and cramped and filthy, it hadn't known
a dusting or an airing out for years.
It had the acid, almost etched-in smell
of three old men who almost never washed.

The byword for cheap around the county,
they raised potatoes, subsisting on them
like the Old Country peasants that they were,
and each fall what they judged they wouldn't eat
they brought to town to sell, decked out in overalls
and red bandanas flaring bright above
the chest hair at the open-button tops
of their faded shirts. And they kept hogs:
not penned but wild, let go in standing corn
to shift for themselves, and the hogs made nests
in the fencerow underbrush, grew tusked and fierce—
they had to hunt them down to take to market.

Wherever the path of least resistance led,
they took it every time. When Willi, now,
the middle brother, died (one winter's end:
it was late February, early March,

and he was at his business in the outhouse
when he had a heart attack, keeled over
with a piece of cornhusk paper in one hand—
they found him there next morning, frozen stiff),
not wanting to fuss around with him
or lay out hard cash for a funeral,
they stood a ladder up against the side
of a half-filled, wire-sided corncrib
and caught him at either end and hoisted him,
bent in the middle like a heavy grain bag,
and pushed him over the top and in.
It seemed to them an adequate solution.
In a couple of weeks, after the thaw,
the neighbors started noticing the smell,
and the sheriff came, and the coroner,
and the body was hauled out, still
in that ludicrous outhouse posture.
Inside of Willi's overalls they found,
pinned in behind the bib, a wad of bills
that came, in worn, dirty tens and twenties,
to a tidy sum of several thousand.

And that was typical of how those three
went about their living and their dying—
pinching the penny first, last, and always,
afraid their early poverty might rise
from the dormant past, demand accounting.
And then it did, when the last brother died.
The estate (the parts of it not recorded
tied up for years in court) was staggering,
most of it consisting of fine land,
and much of that bestowed on nearby towns
for parks, or else on favorite tenants.
The contents of the barns and sheds took up
a whole day at auction. And that was that.

They seemed (and seem) types of their generation:
having climbed, closefisted, up from poverty,
they never learned to handle life's largesse.
How hard it is to reckon in the blessing
ourselves among the ones that we would bless.

Late Autumn Woods

The leaves soak up the last of light,
distilling gold out of the air.
In gusts of wind they hold on tight.

They dance and sway on stems so slight
the woods are fluttering everywhere.
The leaves soak up the last of light.

I gaze and gaze but never quite
can see the leaves come wholly clear.
In gusts of wind they hold on tight.

Still, nothing else is half as bright,
standing far away or near,
as when the leaves soak up the light.

It is a lovely, lively sight;
I almost always stop and stare.
The leaves, in gusts of wind, hold tight.

Somehow it always seems so right
to look up into burnished air.
The leaves soak up the last of light;
in gusts of wind they hold on tight.

Noodler

The one thing you can count on doing this—
folks will think it's strange. And I suppose
for all intents and purposes it is.
They want to know the why of it, but that's
hard to tell someone who's never done it.
But then that's true of almost everything.

It was my old man who got me started.
Stripped to the waist, down to just our shorts,
we'd wade along the bank on either side.
He showed me how to spot a catfish hole
back in beneath an undercut, to tell
the history of the current from a snag,
not to mind the fish's coarse flat teeth
as it clamps down its jaw—those things that make
the whole thing come alive. But I don't know,
it's more than that, much more than that, somehow.

There was a time when we took trophy photos,
Dad and me with channel cats or flatheads,
each arm with a huge fish at the end,
but that became in time an outworn story—
same thing every time except the details,
like trying new positions making love.
It's the love of the person or the thing
that counts—and so it is with noodling.
I can no more tell you how I fell in love
than I can tell what drew me to the water,
made me get in and wrestle out big fish,
except it was a thing my father loved,
and to be like him was then my one great wish.

Well, it's not the same as running trotlines
to feel the water cool around your legs,
your shorts ballooning slightly there around you.
Reaching back in under in the water,
you have no clear idea of what is there.
It could be a snake, or the most aggressive
of the dangers, a beaver, waiting in the hole,
and there are muskrats and even snapping turtles.
But I suppose it's just like anything:
some of the fun is in the risk you take,
and if your luck gives out, you asked for it.

I've seen old-timers, with their gnarled, chewed hands,
some with a short finger, or even short a finger,
and not a one I talked to ever said
he'd trade a moment of his noodling in,
it was that much a living part of him.
Except the hands, I guess I'm one of them.

After Things

The farmhouse, with its windows broken in,
now lets the light in through the roof as well.
The farmer, when he lived, kept up the place
as best he could (at least, till that last spell).
His sense of upkeep didn't run to paint;
the wood was weathered to a soft dove-gray.
About the only color on the place
arrived with spring, the purple lilac blooms
that hung like heavy breaths against the shed.
But gradually I realized he was dead
as one by one some certain signs appeared.
The roof, once new from an insurance claim,
had finally broken in, the slanting light
speckling one upstairs bedroom wall I saw
in driving by, where hail and rain and snow
dropped in from time to time or stayed the night.
The way in to the place had been closed off
with a white-barred swinging gate he now kept locked
("he" being the new owner of the farm).
He worked the land—as close as he would come
to honoring the old guy who was gone.

The thing that spoke most forcefully of him
(I mean the old guy) was the pond that lay
a little down the slope behind the barn.
I used to fish there sometimes after work.
Scrub willow and small bushes lined the bank
on the west and south, and I often stood
where the shallows had no reeds and cast my lure
out toward the trees, as near as I could come,
and watched it splash and shatter its reflection,
and how the surface healed itself again.

I never tired of that, the evening sounds
of meadowlarks and insects, and the sky
full of the roiling flanks of cumulus
or cirrus like a light snow in the spring.

One evening, looking for a spot to try,
I saw a fish roll over just beneath
the surface in a sudden, ghostlike turn,
and I cast toward it, and the plug splashed down.
Almost at once, the water boiled and broke.
I set the hook, and then a bass leaped up,
straightened, and walked the surface on his tail,
the flying droplets catching all the light.
For two or three minutes I fought him there.
He gave it all he had. I horsed him up
onto the bank, a three- or four-pound largemouth,
his gills raking the unaccustomed air.
I had to cut the hook to free him then
and held him while he rested in the shallows.
Then, like a shot, he swam into the depths.
Something about the whole thing made me feel
the old guy was still looking after things—
the only way he could, considering.

Dancer

in memory of Sidna Hazen

How can it be,
she wonders, her heart
goes out to it still,
the single tree out back?
Its apples never came
to much; nevertheless
it goes on bearing,
if only to sweeten the grass.

Some days it's been
a comfort to her.
A mist of buds in spring,
and then the long-drawn
whitening, the petals
poured full of light
much in the way
the dancers' skirts

dazzle the eye
in Degas' paintings.
A dancer, yes: she sees
herself, long-legged girl
of long ago, her skin as pale
as apple flesh, whirling
around in the yard,
making her long dress swirl.

Cover of Darkness

Three sisters, with the ashes of the fourth,
drove out into the country after dark,
the plastic bag inside its cardboard box
not buckled in on one side of the seat.
They turned in at the entrance to the park,
drove for a mile or so, and dowsed the lights.
The lid came lightly up, and lifting out
the bag that had the density of sand
but sifted like fine flour as it swung
light-heavily beside the carrier,
they crossed a swale, stepped over a strand of wire,
and waded up a slope of grass and weeds,
emerging on the golf course where a tee
confronted lesser golfers with a pond.
They had a flashlight, but its cold beam made
only a narrow aisle that blinded them
to everything around; they turned it off
for an approaching car, then left it off.
And each one, with a butter dish as scoop,
reached in to do her part in honoring
the sister's wish. The light wind trailed away
each shake of ashes like a swirl of smoke.
Soon they were in the cottonwoods that rose
beside the pond, the leaves wind-shivering.
By now they were spread out and little more
than voices to each other in the dark,
but never closer than in this final act
of sisterly devotion. Met again,
they stood in silence as the fireflies
drifted and surged along the water's edge,
the small light lapping on the ripples there
like shuttered lanterns, and a time or two
were on the verge of speaking when one flared,
soared unseen beyond them in the air,
and scarred the darkness high above their heads.

New Poems

Wright Morris: *Clothing on Hooks, The Home Place*

(black and white photograph, 1947)

Here the mind that is eager to dismiss,
picking out these items on the wall,
notices a jacket, a sweater and cap,
and is entirely sure that that is all.
But the longer one looks, the more one sees,
and every lesser detail here agrees:
and so we see the wall is pocked and scuffed,
and one end of the cap's bill has been torn,
and the sweater's holes in places show the wall,
and the jacket's tattered denim looks forlorn.
Strange how such clothing, just by hanging here,
speaks of the life of labor it has led,
and the shadow cast by the nail above
leans at an angle, though hit on the head.

Dale Nichols: *Morning Chore*

(oil on canvas, 1972)

The top of the sky's cobalt's reflected here
in lesser blue beneath the foreground's snow,
as though the earth had drawn a line of shadow,
a crystal condensation, from the air.
Light or the lack of it is everywhere
you look, and last week's fall and blow
still lies above the barn's brick-red below.
Nothing in the whole scene seems astir.

But look: below the windmill, bending over
the frozen water tank as for a shot
at pool, the farmer leans to chop the ice
and free the water from beneath the surface.
There are shards floating where his ax has caught.
Each cow will sip her image like a lover's.

Lunching with Friends

in memory of Rosalind Lamson

After the good food, coffee, and good talk,
sitting with our elbows on the table
or leaning back against the backs of chairs,
a momentary lull comes over us.
We share the quiet now; it is enough.
Crumbs loom upon the tablecloth's smooth white
like risen loaves; the one bud in its vase
admits us to the fellowship of light.

Salon Noir, Niaux

That place where the trees turn suddenly to grass
and form a bowl-shaped meadow—it was there
one day we happened on a herd of bison,
a small one, only three or four of them.
Peering out through a screen of ferns, I chose
the nearest one, feeding all by itself,
then signaled Og and Tilloth, and they drew,
their bows bent back and sighted, while I kissed
my arrow so it would fly true, fitted
the notch, drew the tremble from the string.
It sang as I released it; *twang* and *twang*
went the air, as Og and Tilloth followed.
High on the side, beneath the back, mine struck—
then theirs, a little lower. And it sprang,
the bison, and went clattering away
as the whole herd scattered. It maybe ran
a hundred strides before its legs turned out
to one side under it, and down it went.
We slit its throat when we caught up to it.
I think it was my arrow did it in,
the skin around it soaked in deep red blood.

That night, around the fire in the cave,
the dressed-out bison wrapped up in its skin
(except for what we'd eaten), in shadow
the women and children sleeping in their robes,
we men sat talking in small voices there.
It was Og, I think, who made a little song
about the bison, how its flesh sustained us,
how its brave death had gone to give us life,
and when he finished singing, he remarked
how the words of a song were not enough—
they flew up out of hearing like the sparks

the fire throws from sight against the ceiling.
You had a picture in your mind, all right,
but that was private—better a picture
up on the wall, an image that would stay,
something that all could look at and admire
together, at one time. That got me thinking.

Next day, I took some sticks of deep black charcoal
and tried a bison on that large back wall.
Then tried another, a little to the left
and slightly higher. That could be the herd
startled away when our shots hit the bull.
Above the first figure, I started on a third.
I drew in arrows on the first two then—
three on the first bison (the one we killed),
and two on the second. It was strange:
something was guiding my dreaming fingers,
was making not exactly what I'd seen
but a choice among the possibilities,
the animals grazing and about to run,
their flow like water as they turned and ran.
Og had been right; this was better than words.
Another dimension, at any rate:
where the words of his song showed our respect
for the bison we slew, its sustaining spirit,
the drawing could show the thrill that we felt
approaching the kill, when the song trailed off
through the cave, and we could no longer hear it.

In the Clear

That was her name; it seemed a perfect fit.
She stood at fifteen hands when she began
(15, 2 to be exact), a two-year-old
chestnut with a blaze between her eyes,
but no one liked her chances in those days—
no one, that is, but Sames. He saw in her
the local champion she would become.
It was his enthusiasm that convinced
the other trainers right out of the gate,
and when she didn't lose a single race
that year, the public—well, they caught on too.
The odds kept tumbling as her earnings grew.

I guess the thing you'd notice about Sames—
he looked like he knew almost everything.
There was a kind of cocksure swagger to him,
and he endorsed this in the way he dressed,
wearing a different silk shirt every day,
the colors all as bright as racing silks.
One I remember in particular,
a sort of tangerine, so deep an orange
you'd swear that you could squeeze it for the juice.
He often wore a porkpie hat as well
and always chewed the stub of a cigar.
There in the half light of the early dawn
I see him still, a figure in a frieze,
shouting, through a megaphone of hands,
instructions to the kid who worked her out.
He told me once, the first time he saw her
he noticed her economy of motion
and was impressed by it, but also saw
she had no tendency to drift out wide
(or if she did, he said, you'd hardly know it).

Funny how a trainer always sees
the thing or things that set a horse apart.
One time I saw him step back from the rail,
look down at his watch, and simply smile.
That was the closest that he ever came
to telling me how high he rated her.

At first he ran her in the small-purse stakes
at little tracks around the area:
Lincoln, Fonner Park, and Madison,
then later at Ak-Sar-Ben, where one meet
she drew a stable berth beside the great
Who Doctor Who. It could be that success
rubs off, said Sames, and flashed that smile of his.
Myself, I think she didn't need such help.
She had it covered in that stride of hers
and her combativeness, her will to win.
None of the corners cut by other trainers,
especially on those small Nebraska tracks,
were ever used by Sames on any mount—
those whips, for instance, with an electric charge
that crack on contact with a horse's flesh.
He had a knack with horses. He would blow
into one's ear until it tensed and flickered,
then take its muzzle, turn its face to him,
stroke its forehead, look it in the eye.
Then, soft but firm, the way a father speaks
to a pouting child, he would speak to it
in measured tones, almost in cadences,
and usually the horse grew calm for him.
You had to see it, really, to believe it.

That's how he brought this horse of his along,
this filly-apple-of-his-eye. Sames knew

she wasn't ready for the big time yet,
but he was working on her confidence,
believing he could make the horse believe.
He babied her with sugar cubes and apples
and told her what a handsome heart she had.
She'd look at him and seem to understand.

So: the next year, her second season out,
began just like the first; race after race
was hers. Mostly she'd lie just off the pace
and then make up the difference down the stretch.
One jock who often rode against her
said he was always nervous in the lead.
He said she'd slip up on you just like that
when you were running clean, and just like that
was round you in a spray of mud or dust.
He said she was one hell of a good horse.
The pressure built, of course, as she kept winning,
and all that spring she did, into the summer.

And then at Prairie Meadows, near Des Moines,
maybe halfway through the meet: she had won
every race again, won them handily,
when one sweltering hot late afternoon
she went out as the odds-on favorite.
Sames later said that she was just as calm
as she could be, back there in the paddock,
under his hands and voice, and he had thought
that maybe she would run a special race.
As usual she hung back in the pack
until the far turn, when she made her move.
How fluidly she glided then, her easy strides
eating the sifted dirt beneath her hooves,
horse after horse erased behind her charge,
her jock up leaning forward featherlight
above her and the rail posts spinning by
as she swung wide and out into the lead,

when suddenly—oh, God! Sames caught his breath—
her right foreleg had crumpled and she fell
asprawl out to the side while her momentum
carried the jockey, leaning forward still,
into a sudden effigy of flight,
landing on his elbows, tumbling over,
breaking his clavicle as gravity caught up.
All she could do was raise her head against
the agony—a broken cannon bone.
Sames rode out with the vet, leaped from the van,
cradled the filly's head in his vast lap,
leaned over whispering into one ear
as the vet's hypodermic bit her flesh.
She shuddered wildly just before she passed.
He stayed with her like that until the truck
came to cart her off with all his hopes.
That night he cried and cried—for both of them.

Climbing Rose

A rose of spring seen with an even eye
Never betrayed the seer; he leaps the sight
And stands within ineluctable dominions,
Saved in some haven of a sheer delight.
    —Richard Eberhart, "The Supreme Authority of the Imagination"

Look now beyond the rose's opened buds,
their rich profusion here against the wall,
their vivid red renewing brick and mortar
in petals that the lightest touch makes fall:

here, in the light of the late morning sun
of early June, be havened in delight,
enclosed by something more than carpe diem,
by joy itself, however sheer or slight:

look far beyond the petal's curling lip,
the dewdrop nestled in one crinkled fold,
the heady scent that rushes to your nostrils,
the soft red down that burns as you take hold:

far beyond the body's sure dominion,
where all the senses join to make a crown,
let your imagination take the scepter,
and all that is before you will bow down:

bow not in adoration but for joy,
the thing itself, displaced, more wholly real,
reordered, more at one with its own nature—
your being whole, the source of all you feel.

Fern

Raking down
through maple leaves
to the slick black and wet brown

at the bottom,
the layers
that went down first last autumn,

I see the tines
bend and spring
where a single nodule shines,

and quickly
clearing away
an area sown thickly

as rabbit scat
with seed,
the pellets dull on the flat

black ground
of the humus,
I make out, on the background

of the warm
red brick wall,
a draggled, feathery form

unfurling
in the sun now,
like a quill from a scroll's uncurling—

the dark plume
of the first thin frond,
given the sky for head room,

standing up straight
as a cock's tail
on the top rail of a gate.

The Long Rise

for my sister, Kathie

Here is the seep, the desert springs at play,
holding the grit for miles around at bay,
and here the tule christens out of green
the landscape's listening look beneath that sheen,
the water clear and clearing, deepening down,
so clear it seems that nothing here could drown.
Under the cottonwoods' slow hankering breeze
the faintest humming, like a swarm of bees,
and at the far end, where the seep descends
on stairs of rock and by a course of bends
into a lower pool, and several kinds
of ducks bob-apple for their unseen finds,
the water thins to dimples on its way
and fills the air with a fine mist of spray.
And your regard holds steady on it there,
the dance of motes and atoms on the air
as regular as breathing out and in,
where water's going makes a quiet din
and this slow welling leads somewhere at last,
rising into the future from the past.

Flat Water

1 Source

A river's waters gather variously.
This one's begin, far west, as melting snow
on peak and mountainside in Colorado,
the sun's glances turning into runnels
that dart and braid and build up to a spate
come brawling over boulders far below,
the mist shot through with sunlight where it falls.
Then at the mountain's foot the water slows,
comes smoother, gliding, under canyon walls,
opens on red rock, mesquite, piñon pine,
and off now on its gradual descent
eastward across the plains, the water tells
less of its origins with every mile
as transevaporation skims the flow,
the vapor towering to the tops of clouds.
Eventually recycled on the wind,
the hoarded droplets spend themselves anew,
high in the mountains, in fresh falls of snow.

2 Past

"Flat water" translates these three syllables,
Nebrathka, a whole state wrested from its namers.
The shame of it still sounds here in the current,
the softly gliding water's roils and dimples,
the channels curved and braided round the sandbars
like a warrior's plaited hair. Flow softly, then,
bright waters, round your bends and glaring stretches,
over the quicksand reaches of your shallows,
your snags and treacheries, who are yourself
much fallen from your great days as a sea,

when the trilobite set down your history
in whorls of stone, your chiseled sediments:
have a care now for your legacy of cranes,
kind mother of a longer-standing care
than any human naming: flow softly there.

3 Promise

I raise this glass of water to my lips
from wells beneath your passage, deep in sand.
It is clear, clean-tasting, and has traveled far,
through time and human history, the past
immediate in every sip I take.

Where might these molecules have started out?
They are the thirst's equivalent of light,
millennia upon its journey here
to greet the eye, from some faint, pulsing star.

In the mind's eye I kneel beside a spring,
the flash of water cold around my hands,
whose open palms are joined to form a cup
that will not hold. Look, between my fingers
the water dives back as I lift it up.

Recede, then, waters, and rise up again.
Here at the tap or on some mountaintop
far west of here, a constant Ararat,
keep faith with us in sending us the Platte.

Four Observations

The soybean harvest's all but cleared the field.
A combine's parked beside what's left to go.
No telling passing by how great the yield.
The dust has settled back like heavy snow.

The Sign Said

"Big Sale 3/4 Mile"—an arrow loosed
or finger pointed down a country road,
the gravel brimming in the morning light—
and yet I did not turn there.

More than the farm machinery, odds and ends
of household furnishings and other junk
that would await me if I went to see,
I called to mind an image

of when the place had prospered long before
and fields ran green with winter wheat in spring,
the dust above the combines gathering
the pouring, sheer gold harvest.

Better to give a long look down that road,
imagine turning in beneath tall trees,
finding a place among the other cars—
and keep on driving westward.

Grounders

When I came crying home that Saturday
from the graveled playground just across the street
where a bad-hop ground-hit ball had caught me
smack in the mouth as I stooped to glove it,
my father rose up from his easy chair,
put down his magazine, and told me
to get the ball that he and I played catch with
and meet him in the alley out in back.

He was waiting for me when I got there,
and on the rough crushed rock he threw me grounders,
time after time for what then seemed forever,
teaching me the fielder's crouch whose purpose
was just to block a bad bounce with my body.
Each time one caromed off, he was elated.

Seventh-Grade Art

Out of a bar of soap I've carved a camel.
It has two humps, is maybe three inches tall.
It can stand on its own four feet,
has that much of the real about it,
though the face and slope of the flanks
have to be taken on faith.
In five minutes I must hand it in,
arrayed in its imperfections,
as if I took a goad and touched its sides
until it rose at one end from the knees
and stood up shakily, tassels dancing,
light bells tinkling on its reins.
Come, camel, let us cross the sands,
the blazing sands that shift beneath our feet
to see if we can find, in waves of green,
the far oasis of approval,
that place where water plashes from a spring
and feeds the roots of date palms
and small ferns. Stand here on my desk
until I give the word.

          Across the empty seat
between us now, Marv Huppolt leans.
"Care if I look at it?" he asks.
He lifts it lightly from the scarred wood of my desk,
transfers it from the fingers of one hand
into the cupped palm of the other.
"Neat," he says. And then, before my eyes,
the S.O.B. proceeds to snap,
one leg at a time, my camel's four thin legs.
He hands it back to me in pieces,
then pokes the friend beside him, and they laugh.

Tears burn, a flash of water choked with sand,
somewhere behind my eyes. The oasis
throbs in the air, becoming a mirage.
My hopes recede like hills of sand behind me.

Remember Me

I don't mean that as a question, the kind
of thing someone comes up to you and says,
say, at a class reunion, and of course
you do, in an odd sort of way, never
having known him or her back in the day
to speak of, and yet something about them,
the way the person stands or holds themselves,
begs recognition now, if not the question,
and of course I mostly don't. The faces,
yes, almost always I recall the face,
but often I can't put a name to it.
But names suggest themselves, and I wonder
how accurate my intuition is.
Sometimes not very. Sometimes the thread insists,
and so I garble the pronunciation,
mumbling something out beneath my breath.
No, what I mean is more a sort of plea,
most eloquent if never said outright,
something furtive in the eyes, almost expectant,
almost petitioning: "*Remember* me."

Kingfisher

for Christof

That breakneck plunge
from a bare tree limb,

the beak extending
into clear shallows,

the fingerling now
a part of him.

Lowbush Clusters

for Evan

Like small green bonnets or swung bells
the berries glisten in the sun.
They'll turn the blue their green foretells,
frosting over as they swell.

At the Station

The air beside the rails abandoned now,
you shuttle round the bend into the dark.
I will drive home and fall asleep beside
the outline of your absence in the bed,
already missing you before you're there.
Waking, I will miss you everywhere.

In the Ted Kooser Contemporary Poetry series

Darkened Rooms of Summer: New and Selected Poetry
Jared Carter

Rival Gardens: New and Selected Poetry
Connie Wanek

The Woods Are On Fire: New and Selected Poems
Fleda Brown

Regular Haunts: New and Previous Poems
Gerald Costanzo

Carrying Water to the Field: New and Selected Poems
Joyce Sutphen

The Track the Whales Make: New and Selected Poems
Marjorie Saiser

Produce Wagon: New and Selected Poems
Roy Scheele

To order or obtain more information on these or other University of
Nebraska Press titles, visit nebraskapress.unl.edu.

Lightning Source UK Ltd.
Milton Keynes UK
UKHW011823230222
399129UK00001B/79